This handy guide to finding sea glass outlines the basics you need to get started.

Tips on when and where to look, what to look for, and how to care for it are included. Filled with beautiful photographs of naturally tumbled Nova Scotian sea glass, this book is sure to inspire the young and young at heart alike.

I'd like to thank my family and friends for supporting me in my seaglassing adventures.

A special thank you to Aaron, for helping me when I am in over my head.

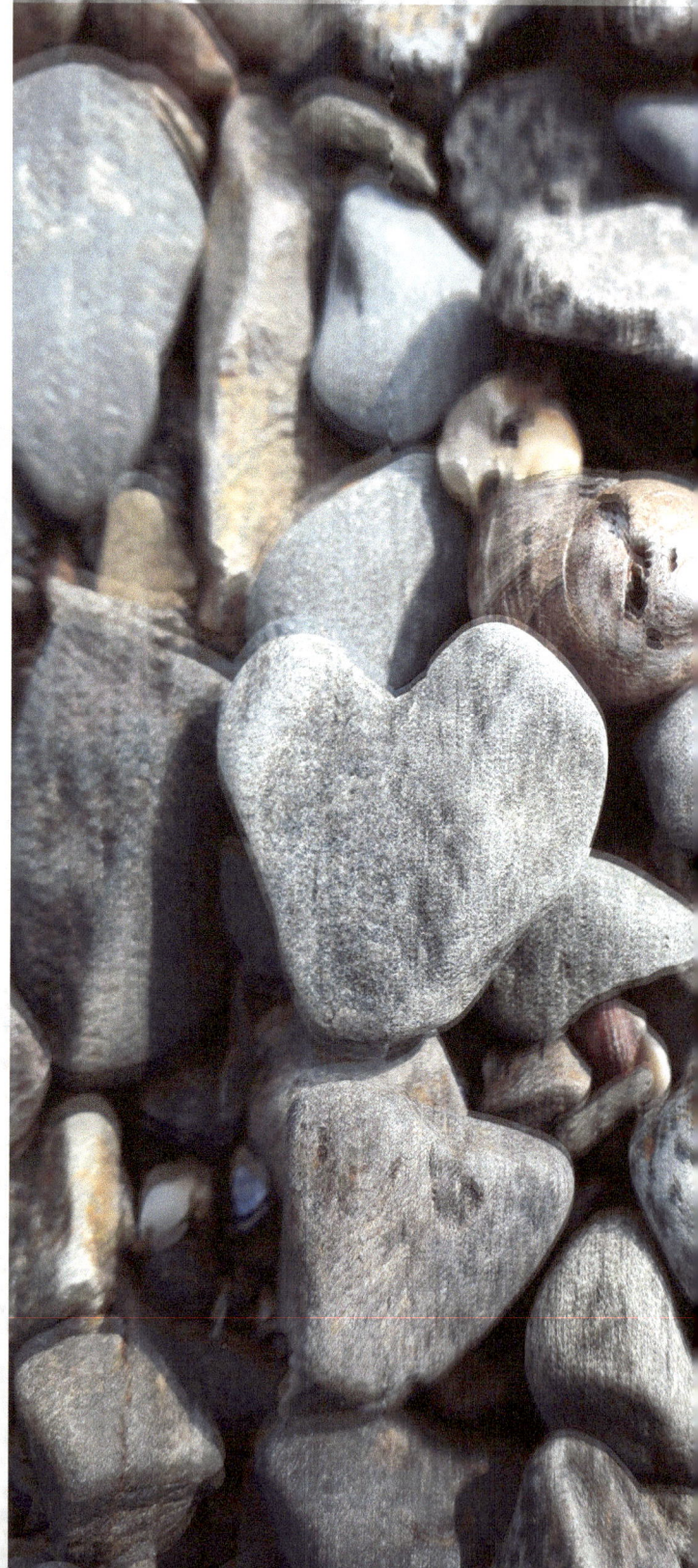

Where I Find My Sea Glass
Beachcombing Nova Scotia

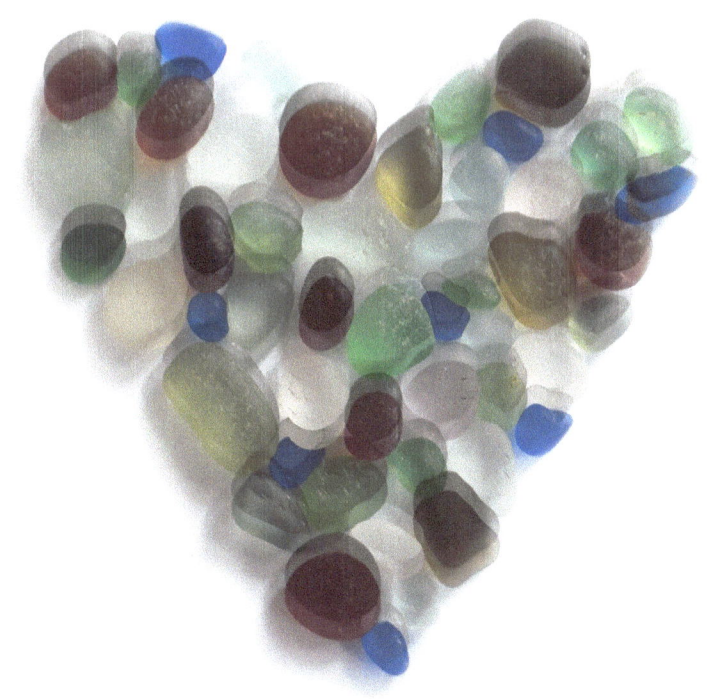

ISBN: 978-1693410680
Copyright 2019 © Kristina Noel

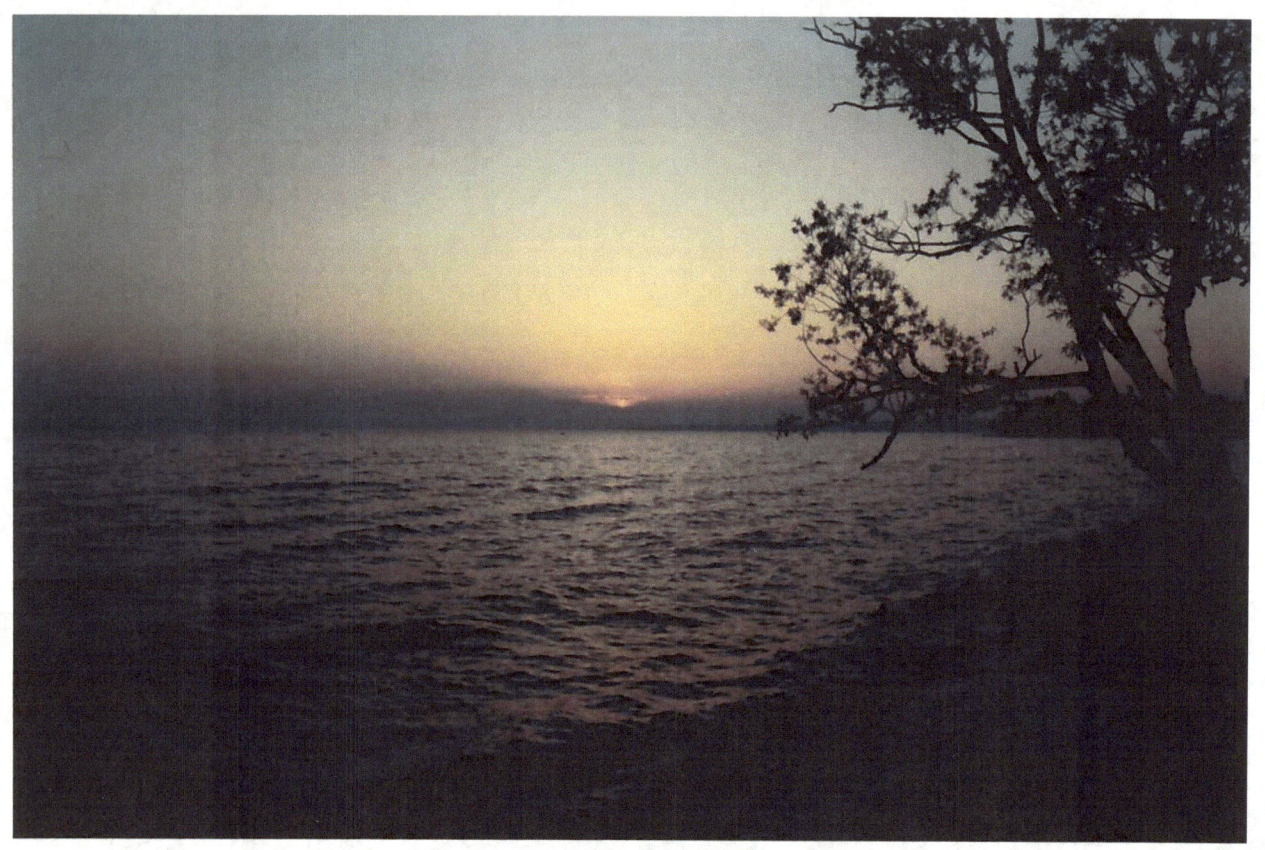

The first time I came across beach glass was about ten years ago, on the northern shores of Lake Nipissing in Ontario, Canada. The pieces were small, common coloured, and not well tumbled. Today I wouldn't get so excited by them, but to me at that time, it was finding something special.

I was amazed at how they caught the sunlight, shimmering under the water like small jewels spilling from an open chest. I brought those little bits home, overjoyed and full of ideas of how I might use them. I was falling in love, with no idea how big the adventure would become.

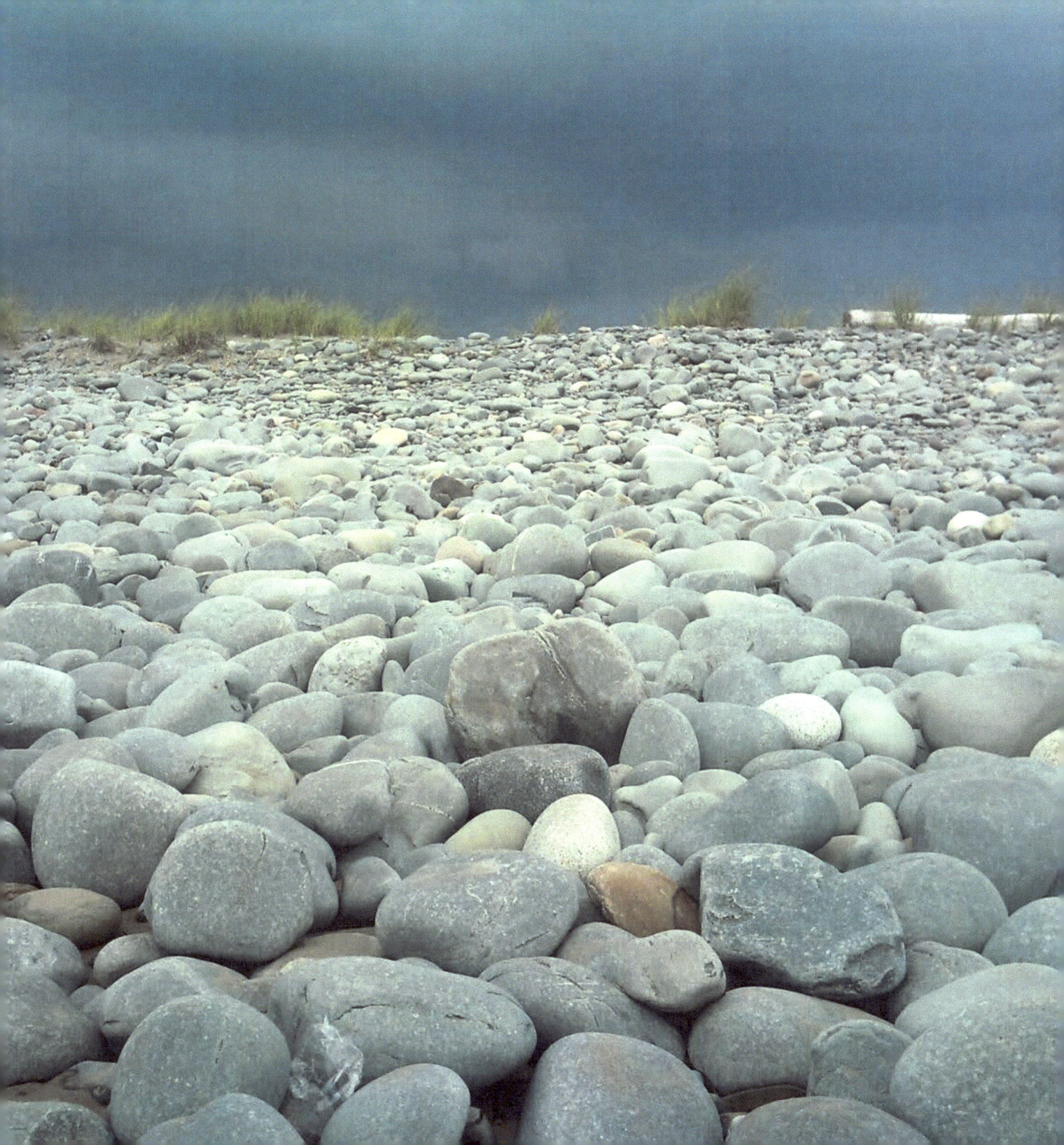

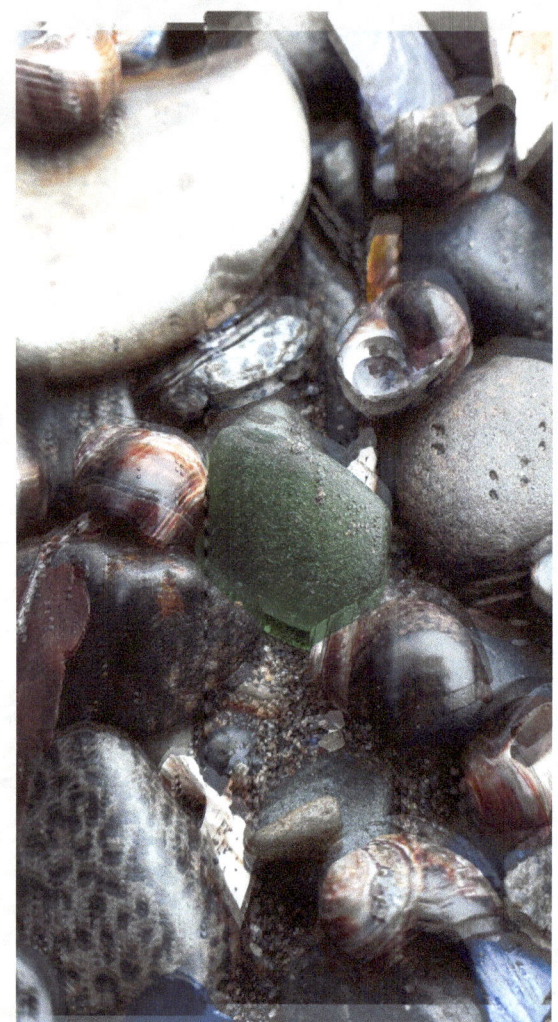 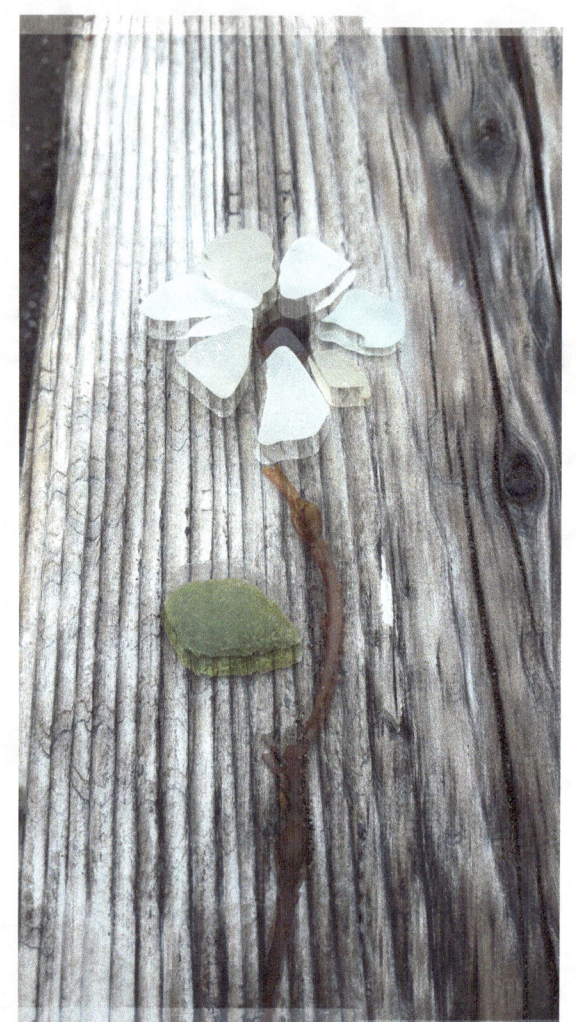

Soon after, my husband Aaron joined the Canadian Forces and our family relocated to Halifax Nova Scotia. For the first time I was living by the ocean and I fell in love with it. It was only a matter of time before I met other glassing enthusiasts.

One of the first things that I learned was that those who love seaglass, love it a lot. They love the hunt, the ocean, and everything about it.

I found out that glass found in fresh water is physically tumbled by the waves or currents, and is called beach or river glass. When the weathering comes from salt water, it is chemically and physically altered due to the salinity of the ocean, as well as the tumbling of the tides, and is called sea glass.

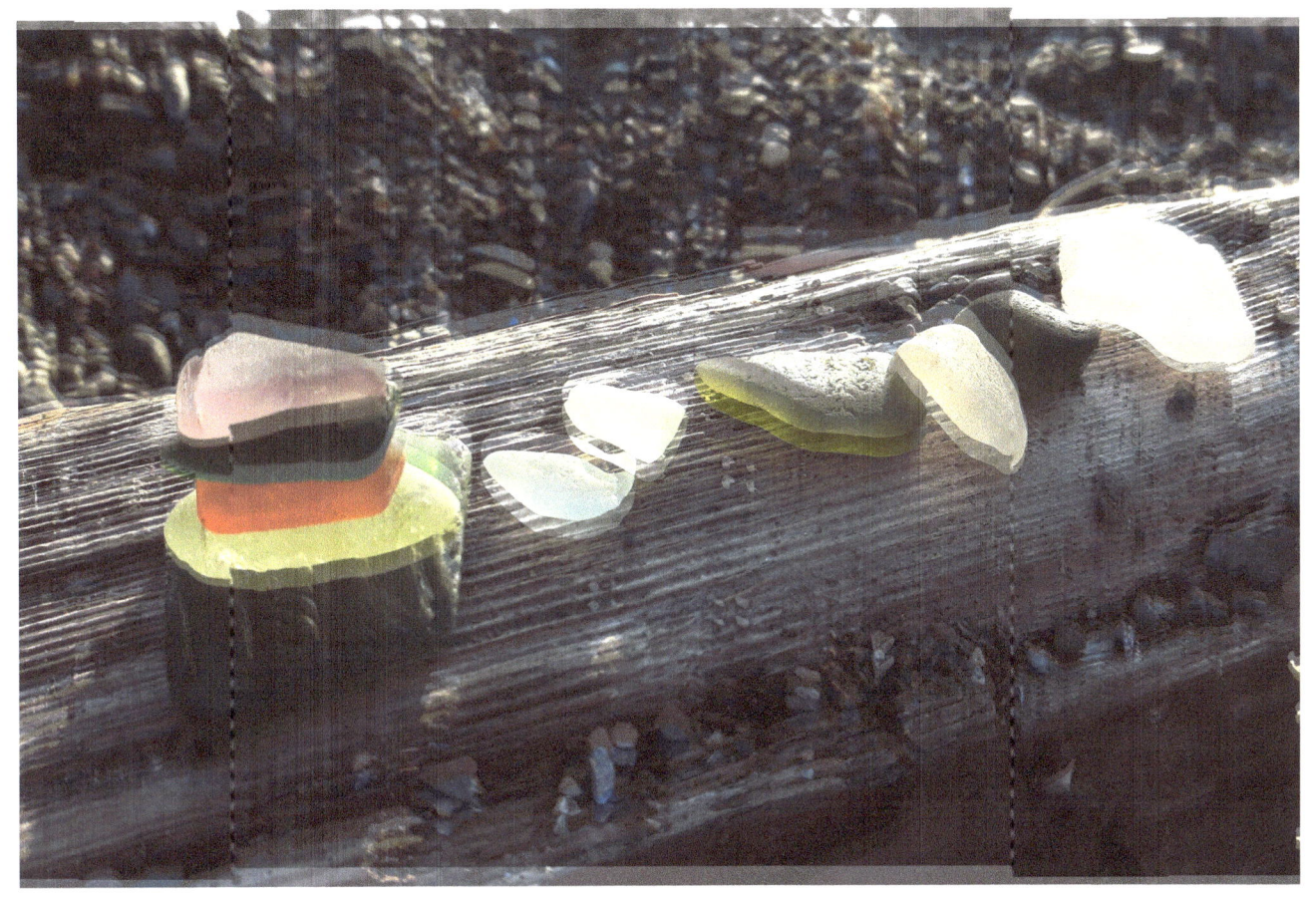

When looking for sea glass, you can go by yourself, or with a friend or two. I enjoy both, depending on the day and my mood.

Many people find hunting alone is their preference. In solitude, with the constant washing of waves across the beaches, we find our peace. Some time to yourself can lift you up, recharging your energy and quieting the mind. Thoughts drift when there is no need for words or focus, and really, it's just really nice to not think for a while and not to have to make conversation, or divide your attention from what you are doing.

If you are going out alone, make sure someone knows where you are and when you expect to be back; beaches shift and change all the time, and tides can trap you if you aren't paying attention. Leave enough time to get back before sunset, as navigating wet rocks in the dark is a sure fire recipe for a turned ankle.

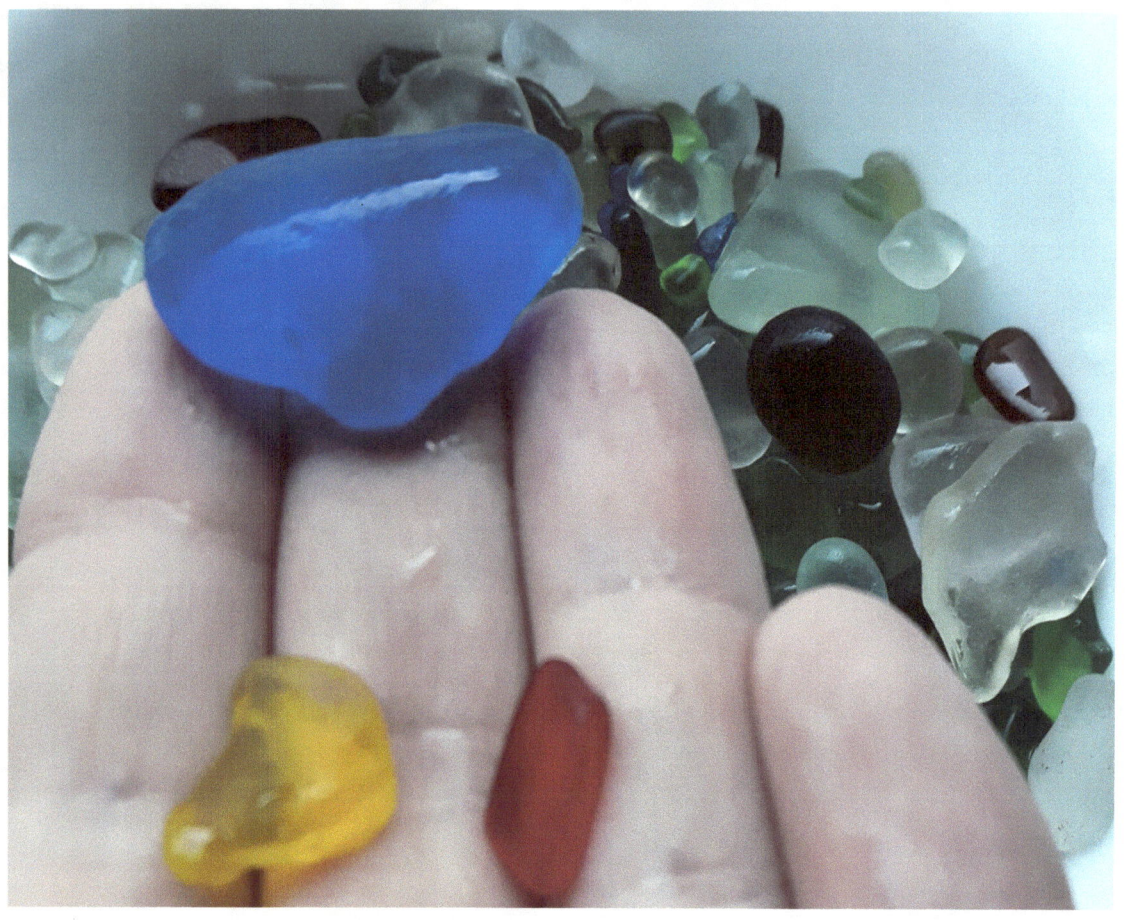

On the flip side, are those amazing, crazy, funny moments that come through shared joy and understanding. It is a blast to go on a road trip to find new beaches, or to have someone to chat with, who really understands your passion.

When you whoop and holler, because after a day on your bad knee, digging and sifting through gravel beds and getting soaked, you have discovered a red beauty, or found your first marble, it helps if there is someone getting excited along with you. I also find it makes you look slightly less silly!

Or when your usual trusty beach isn't producing, they say *"screw it, let's hit the thrift stores while we are here together."*

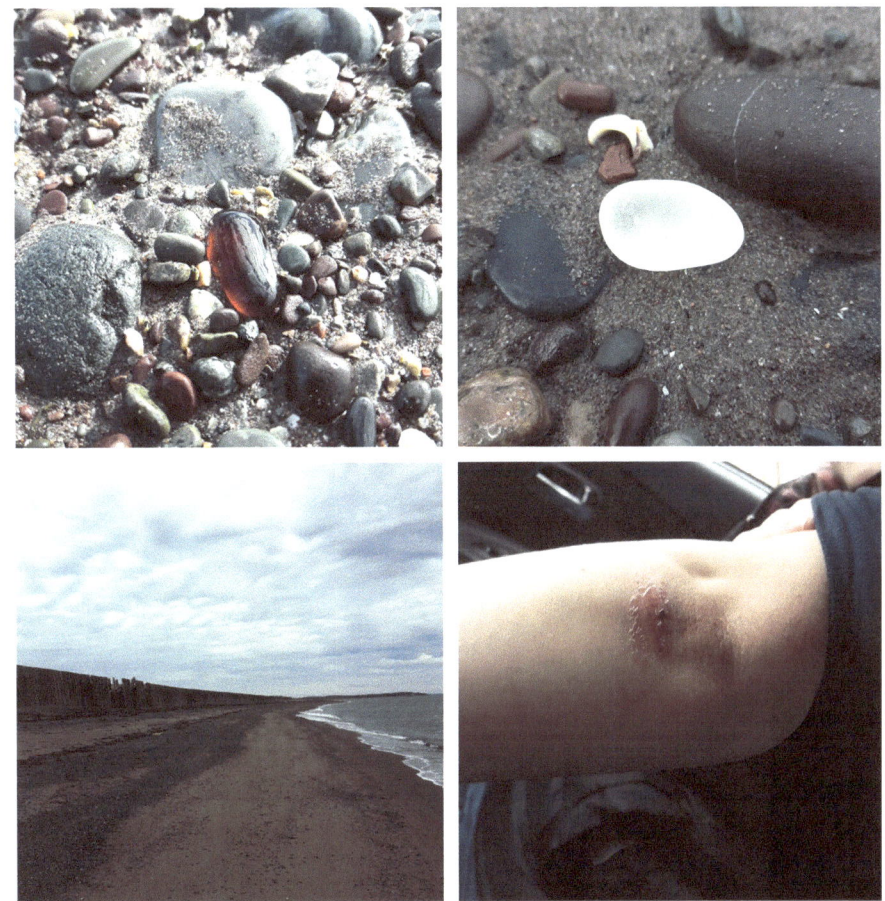

It is also safer, in general; unless the person you are with talks you into shortcuts, side quests, explorations of ruins, climbing down rickety tracks, etc. Disclaimer: I usually am that 'bad idea that sounds good' person.

I love exploring shorelines to find new spots, but it often entails a lot of hiking and climbing, so it is a good idea to have sturdy footwear. It may seem crazy to climb down crumbling hills, or go under big boulders, but often that is where overlooked beauties are hiding.

Don't try a risky spot when you are alone and watch for falling rocks.

Just remember it is easier to climb down than up, but you can get hurt going down too!
I jumped down off of a breakwater, knocking my elbow in the process, not a great way to start the day. It was worth it... I think.

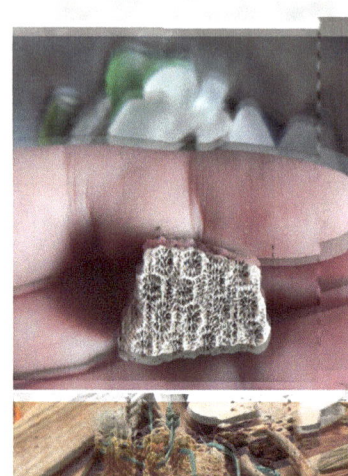 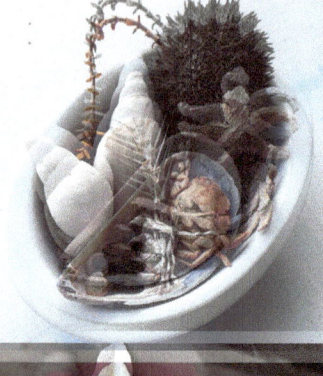 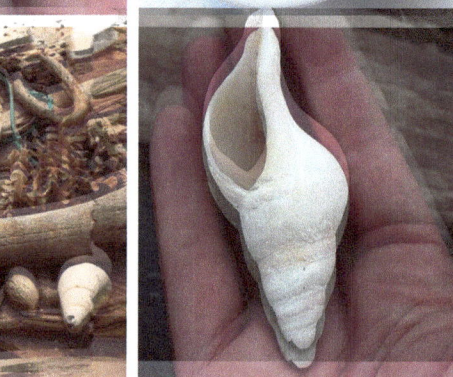 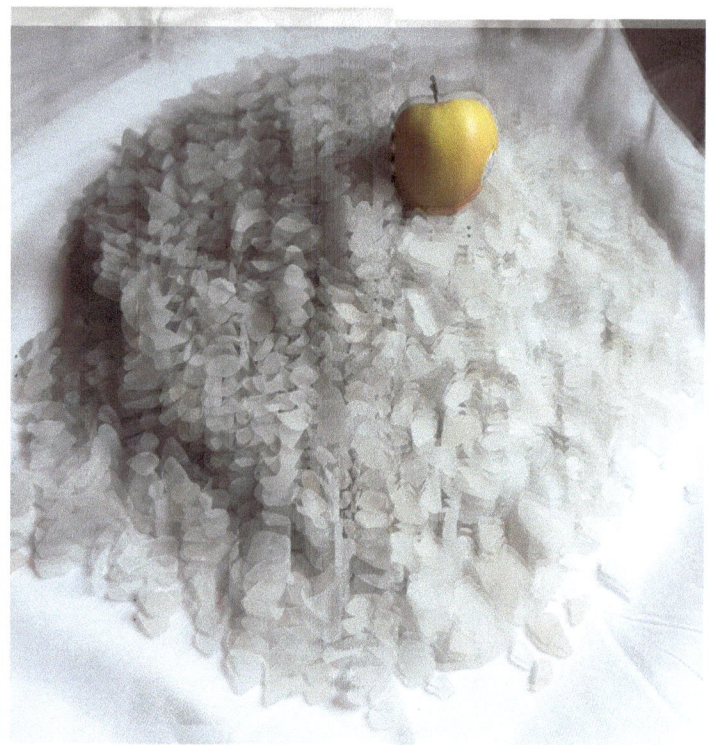

When I first began searching for sea glass, I had no idea what I was doing, and as to be expected, my results were pretty hit or miss. I didn't know what to look for, when trying to find a good sea glass beach and to be honest, I wasn't sure about what was a keeper, and what should be left.

If it was glass and not super sharp, or a pretty shell, or stone, or a cute bit of driftwood, it came home with me! Of course, it didn't take long until I had big mounds of sea debris about the house, and someone telling me I needed to do something with it, or stop bringing it home.

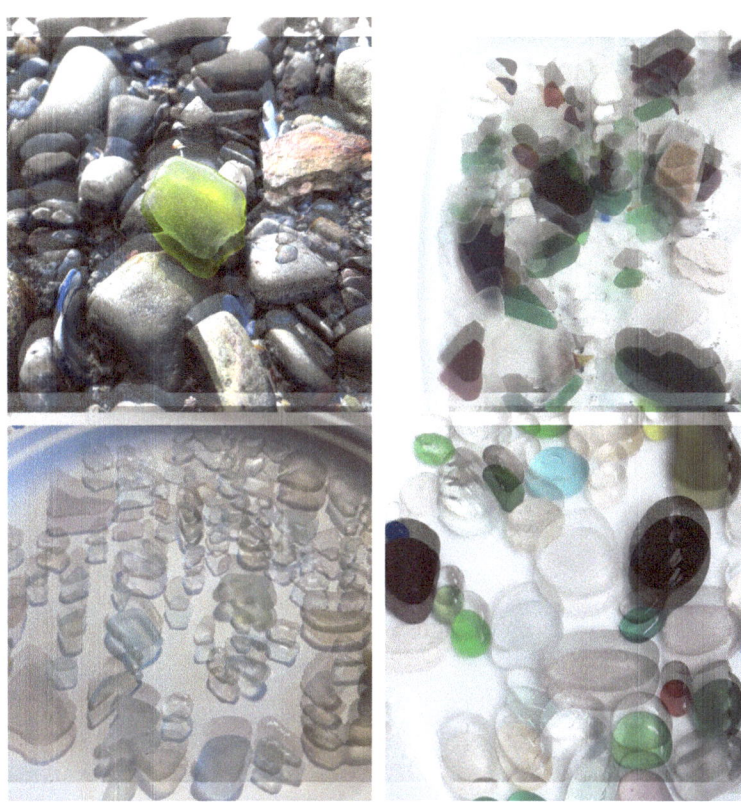

Speaking of bringing it home, cleaning your finds is an important step. The ocean is not a clean place, and though you may not see it, there can be all sorts of contaminants on your glass. I start with a wash in cold water, changing it twice, then a third time with a squirt of dish detergent which helps breakdown oils. Separate out any shells you may have picked up, as they can not handle bleach or CLR. After rinsing, I soak it overnight in cold water and green bleach, rinsing again well with cold water.

As a final step, I soak it in CLR and water overnight, then thoroughly rinse with cold water. This way everything on the sea glass is gone, the true colours are revealed, rust is lifted off and algae stains are removed.

This is actually a 'white piece! Many times I have soaked my 'white' glass to find all sorts of pastels.

Driftwood is easiest to bleach in a bathtub with water and green bleach, soaked overnight. I try and put it out to dry in the sun, turning a few times a day, until it is dry.

Sea glass hunters will talk with you about hunting for it for ages, in a roundabout way, making sure not to give up their special spot. Asking someone where they found their seaglass can get really awkward. It's the equivalent of asking a fisherman where his best fishing hole is, and can be seen as bad manners.

Therefore, it helps to know how to find a good beach for yourself, even if you are in an area that is new to you.

As I spent more time beachcombing I learned a lot, though often the hard way. I began to see it made sense to check the tide times, so I wasn't trying to hunt on a beach that was underwater. I try to arrive at least 2 hours before low tide to have enough time to search properly.

Traveling to areas where there have been fishing wharves, ferry docks, parks, old dump sites or historical locations increased the chance of finding good stuff. I also found out that you can burn a lot of gas trying to find beaches, so it's best to map them out online first.

Beaches change with every tide, as gravel and boulders move about, and storms can change them drastically. What was once an average beach can become bountiful with unexpected beauties.

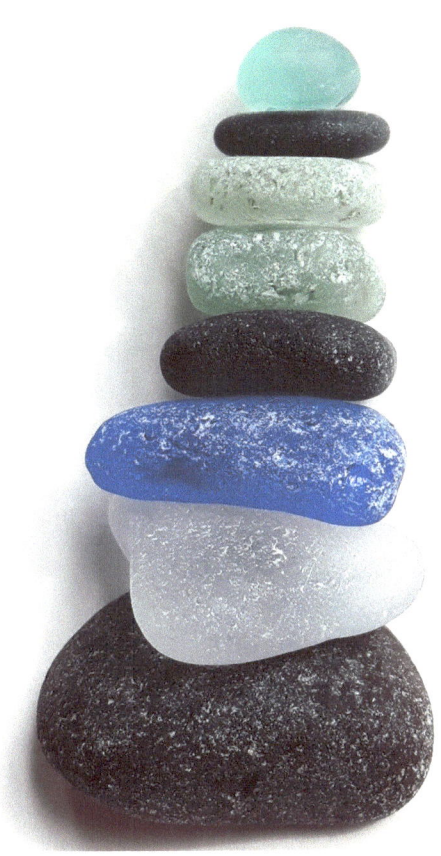 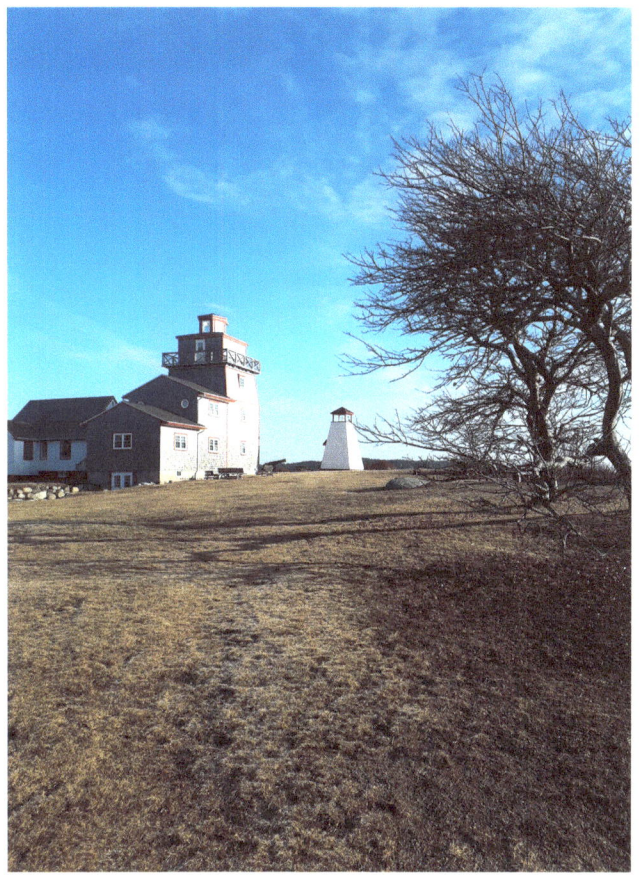

When I am on the beach, I search in a series of passes back and forth parallel to the shore, paying special attention to gravel mounds and rock piles. I flip over smaller rocks as sea glass can be wedged beneath. I bend pretty far down, or sometimes even sit right down, to get a good close view. It can be easy to miss pieces, so making more than one pass gives a better chance for it to catch you eye under different light conditions.

I have a small hand rake I use after storms, for moving mounds of seaweed, or jellyfish that wash up.

I also bring a pair of rubber coated gloves, in case I need to haul a mucky log, or lift up rocks.

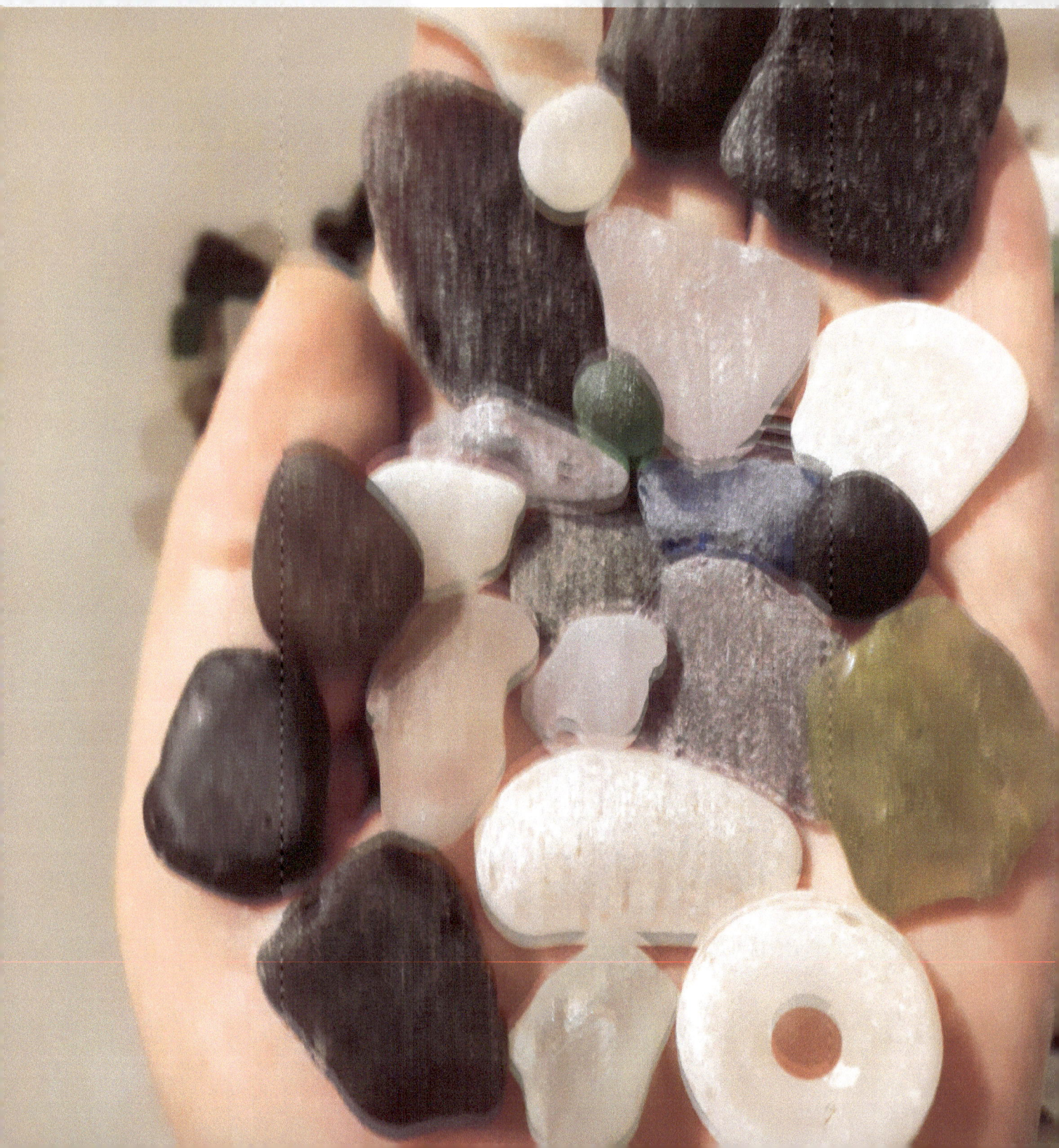

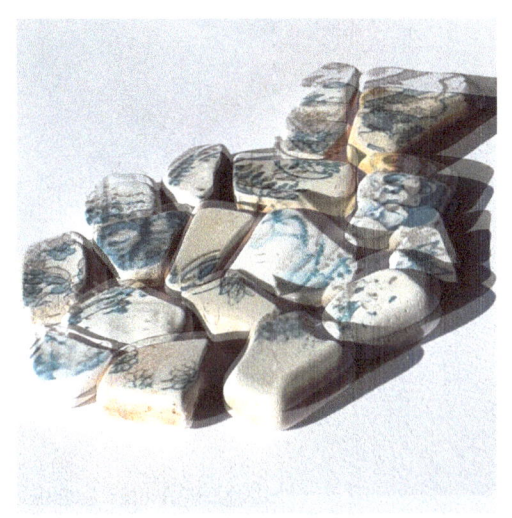 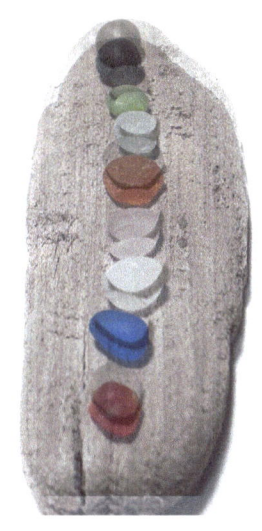 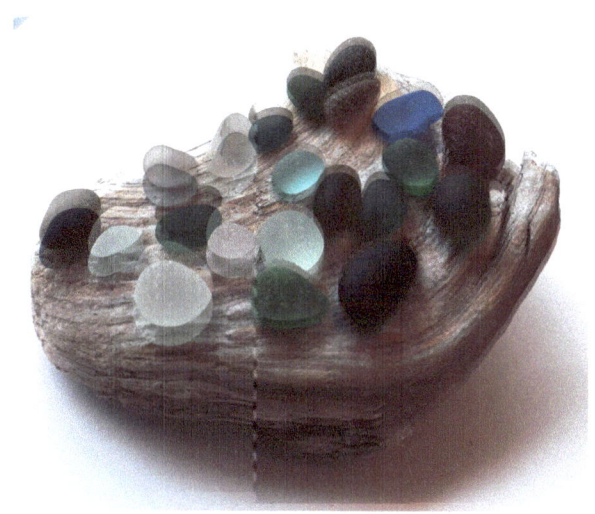

I eventually learned not to bring home every single bit of glass I found. If a piece of sea glass isn't ready, I leave it, unless it is a really rare colour, in which case I usually want to bring it home to get a few good shots with my camera.

Sea glass needs time to form, decades at a minimum, to allow the sea to naturally tumble it and for the salt to do it's work. Over time, what started out as a broken bottle, vase, glass ashtray, plate or jug, becomes a smooth, rounded piece of sea glass or sea pottery. The rolling of the waves through sand and rock breaks it down, and the acidity of the ocean begins to form a rind on it, giving it a frosty appearance when dry. Small knicks on the surface form the classic "C" shaped marks.

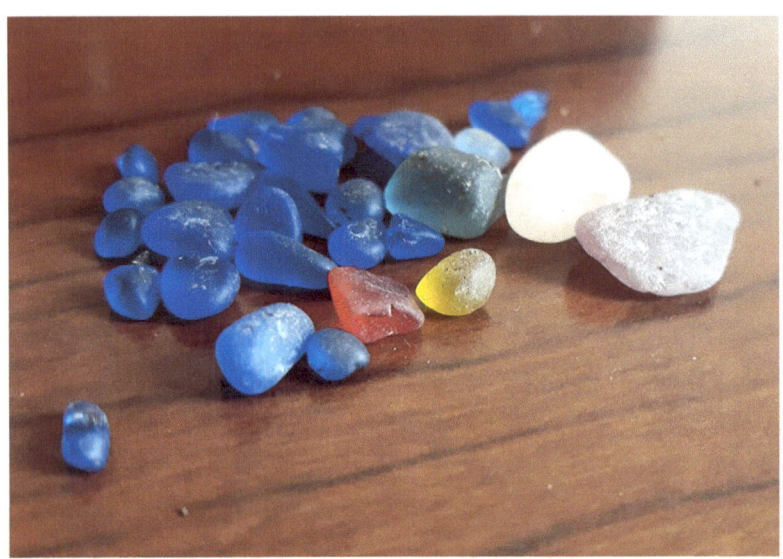 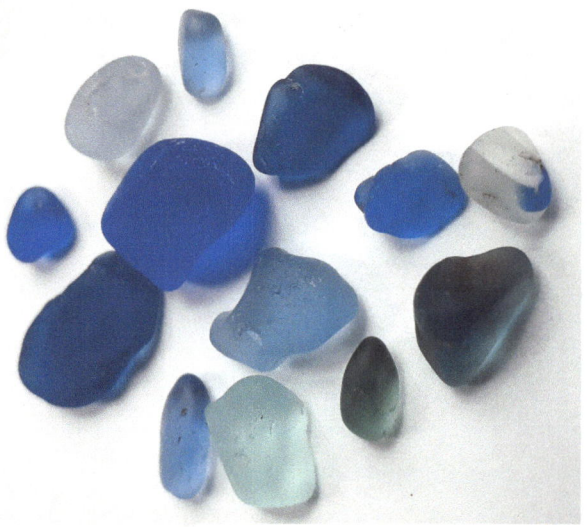

I was always on the hunt for a rare colours like blues, reds or oranges or hoping to find my first marble and was curious as to why there are marbles some places and not others, and why they were there in the first place. It turns out that there are four main reasons.

The first, and unfortunately becoming most common reason, is that someone seeded them. Seeding is when someone intentionally dumps glass or objects like marbles at the beach, to turn them into sea glass. Because it takes so long for it to form naturally, these pieces are easy to spot as they have no wearing or softening.

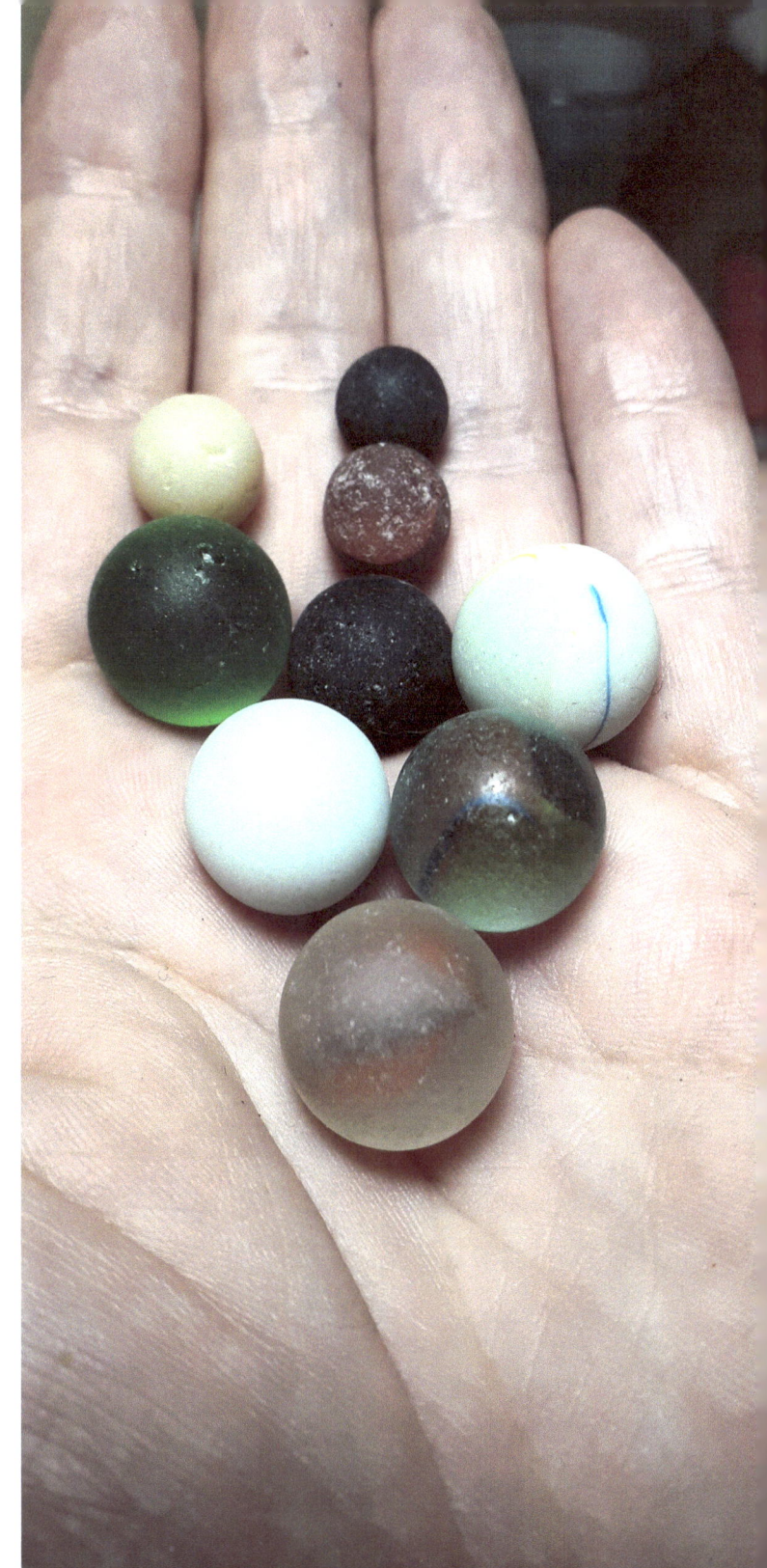

The second way they end up there is through sling shots. People would play with them at the beach, seeing who could shoot the furthest. Sadly, there are less fun reasons as well, from those who used them to chase off birds.

Thirdly, they were used in paint cans, to mix the colour, and ended up in dump sites which were often located right by the ocean. Over time, the dump site erodes away into the sea, by which time the paint can has rusted away, leaving behind the marble. It ends up washing in the sea for a few decades, and becomes someone's treasure.

The fourth reason was pop bottles. Back in the day, Codd soda bottles were made to have a marble in the neck to help with carbonation, and when these bottles broke, the marble was released. These classic aqua coloured marbles are known as Codd marbles.

There have been theories as well that plain clay marbles, made in Germany and the US were used as ballast on ships, and were sold at the destination, although there is not much record of it.

The brightly coloured glass marbles, of the childrens toy type, were not used as ballast in ships.

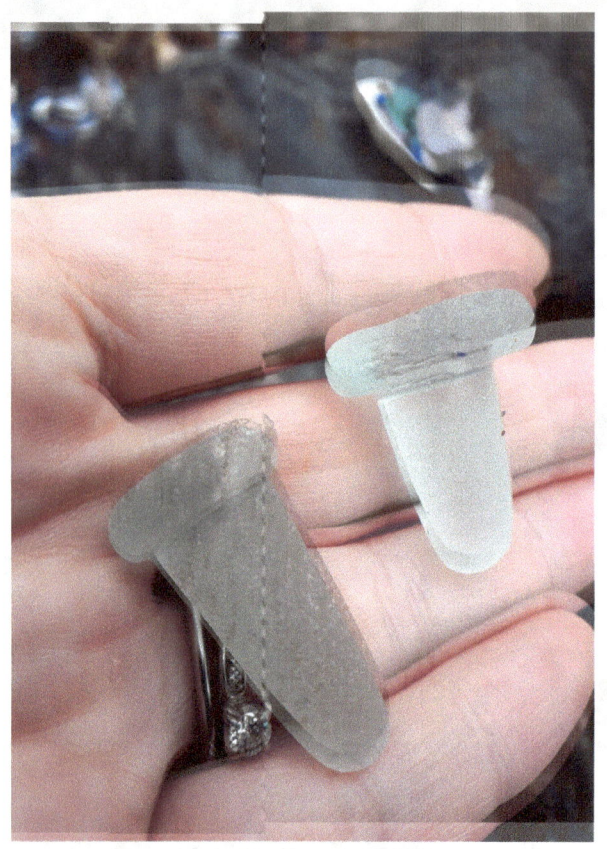 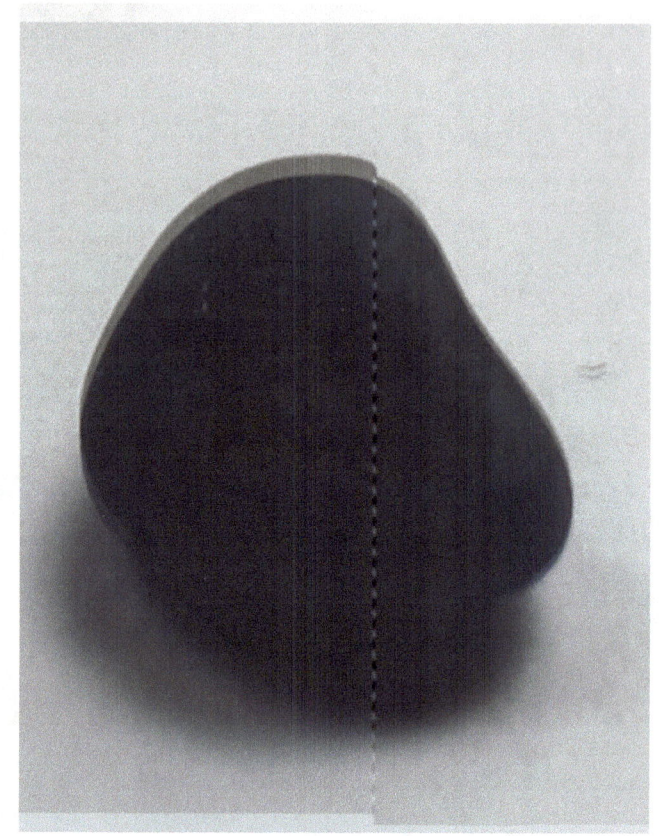

Finding rare colours can be the thrill of a lifetime, sea glass wise:

The most common colours are white, brown and green, and they account for roughly 65% of the seaglass.

The next 30% are aquas, sea foam, lavenders, milk glass, and olive colours.

The final 5% are the rarest colours like cobalt blue, cornflower blue, red, yellow, orange, teal, grey, peach, pink, purple, opalescent, or multi coloured.

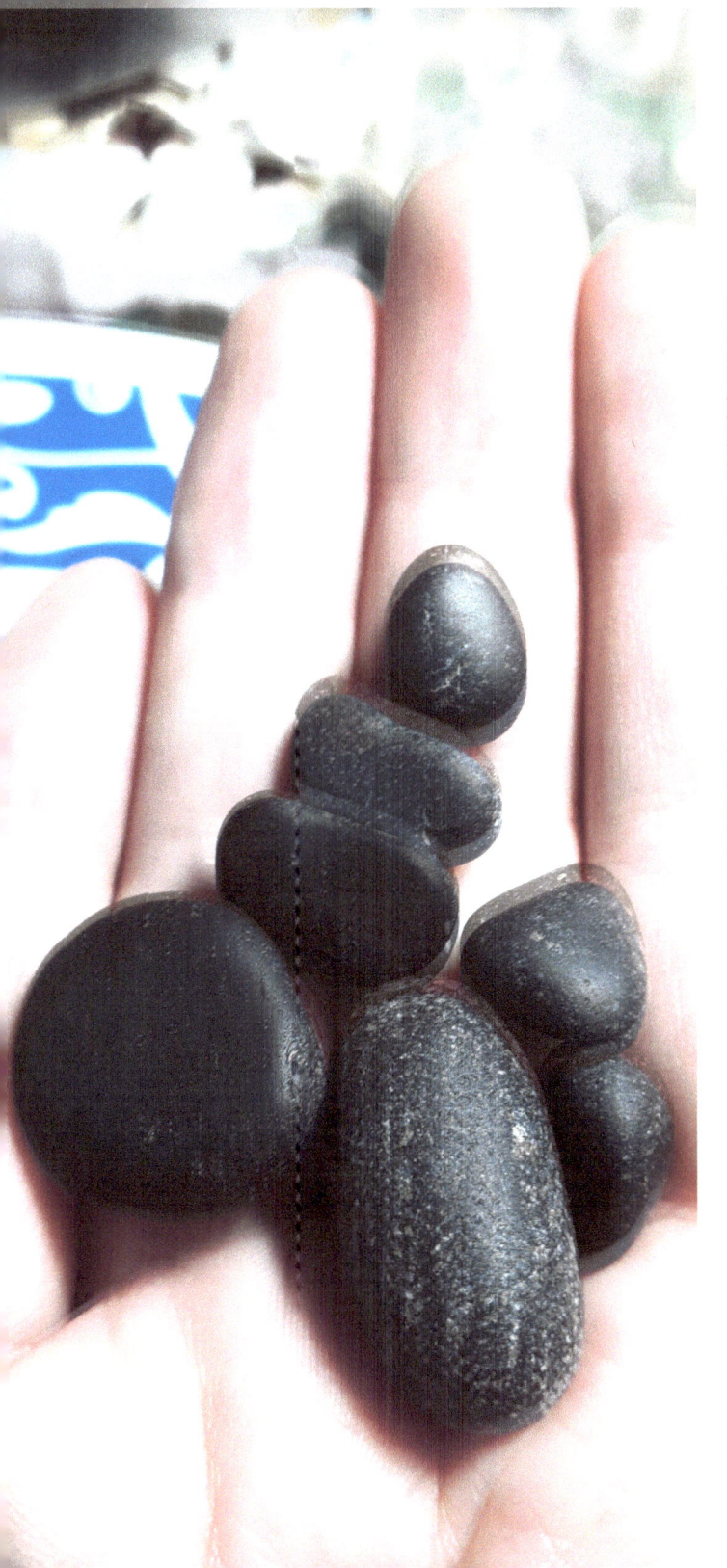

People talk about black seaglass, but it isn't actually black, it just looks that way because the light shining through it isn't strong enough to penetrate.

When glass was produced in the past, it sometimes had iron slag added to strengthen it and make it more robust as it had to last much longer and be used in all conditions. It held up well in shipping, and also lasts as bigger chunks once becoming sea glass. This caused the glass to be much darker, thicker, and the effect makes it opaque and can appear black.

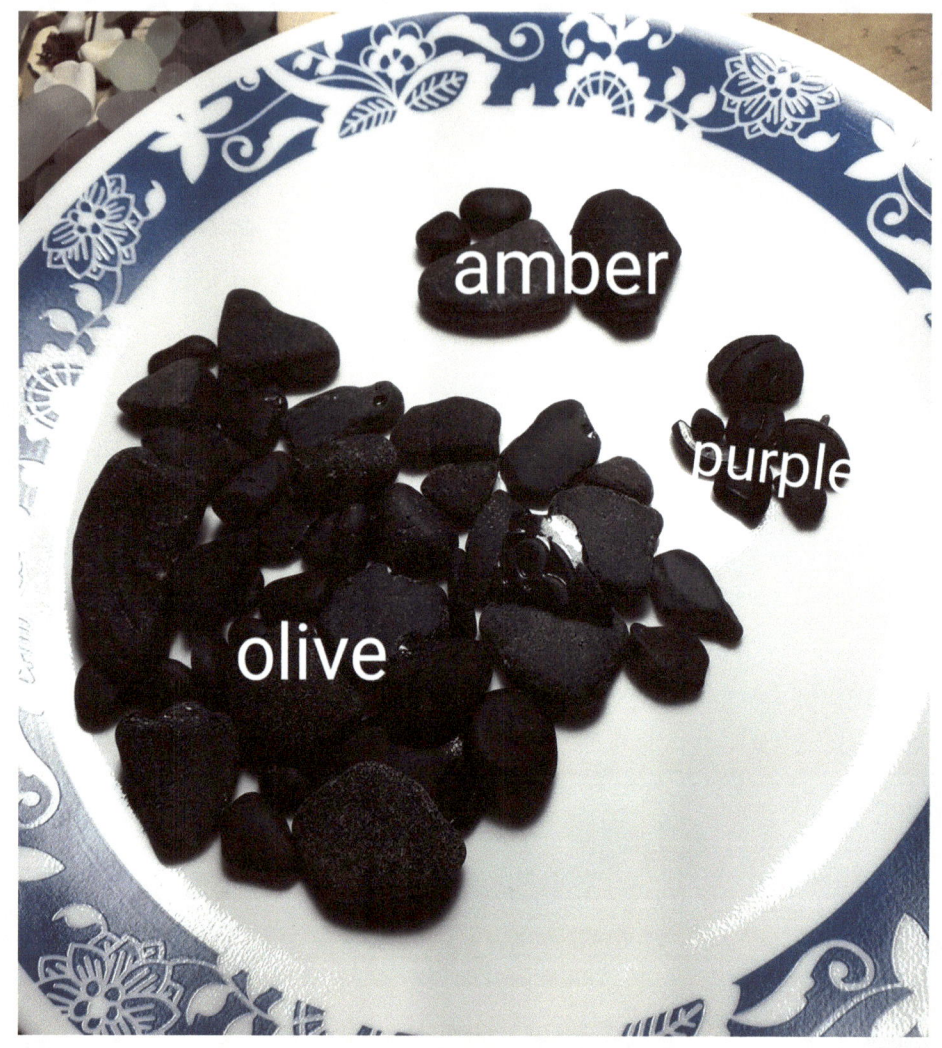

If you can find a light strong enough, eventually you will find it was deep green, blue, red, purple or brown. If it appears red or purple, it may be cranberry glass which had gold salts added to it in production. These cranberry glass dishes and ornaments were very popular for a time in the Victorian era.

When these pieces of 'black sea glass' are on shore, they are very easy to overlook, as they can look just like rocks.

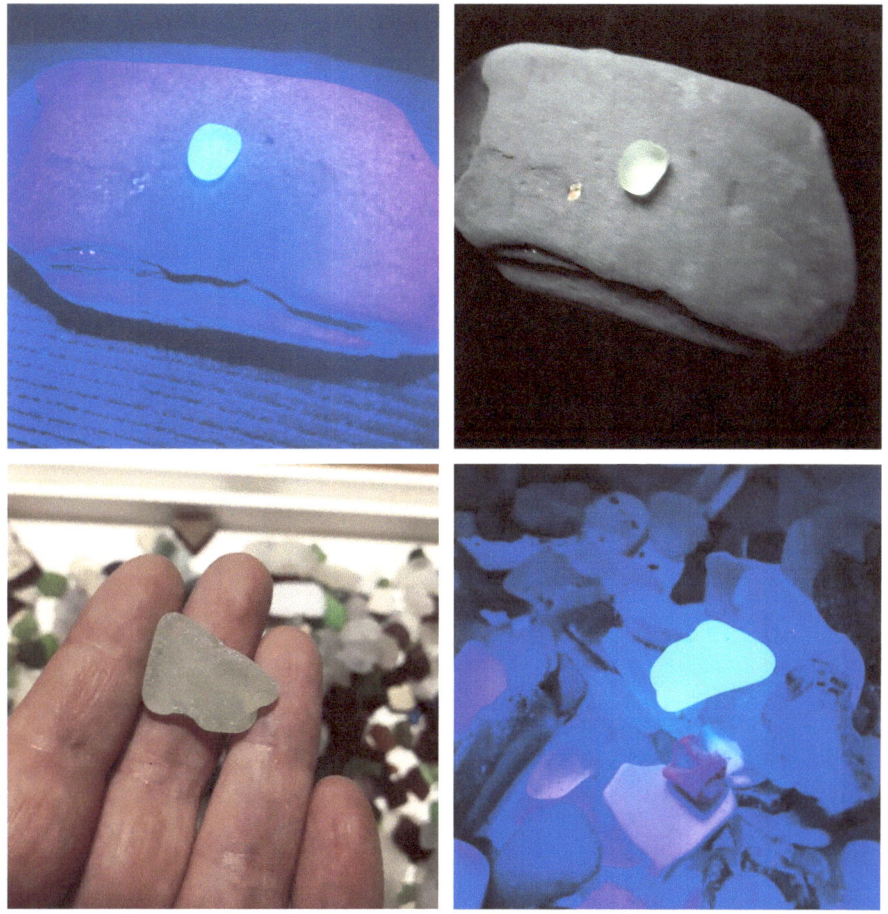

One of the wildest things for me was discovering that under a black light, some sea glass and pottery will glow! Vaseline glass and green Depression glass from pre 1930's had small amounts of uranium oxide added to it, that react to uv-light and give the classic yellowish green glow in the dark colour that we are all familiar with.

Sometimes it was used in pottery glazes as well, so it is worth checking out your sea pottery along with your regular sea glass.

Other additives like selenium, chlorophyll, cadmium, and manganese oxide can create glowing reds, oranges, violets, blues, pinks and more.

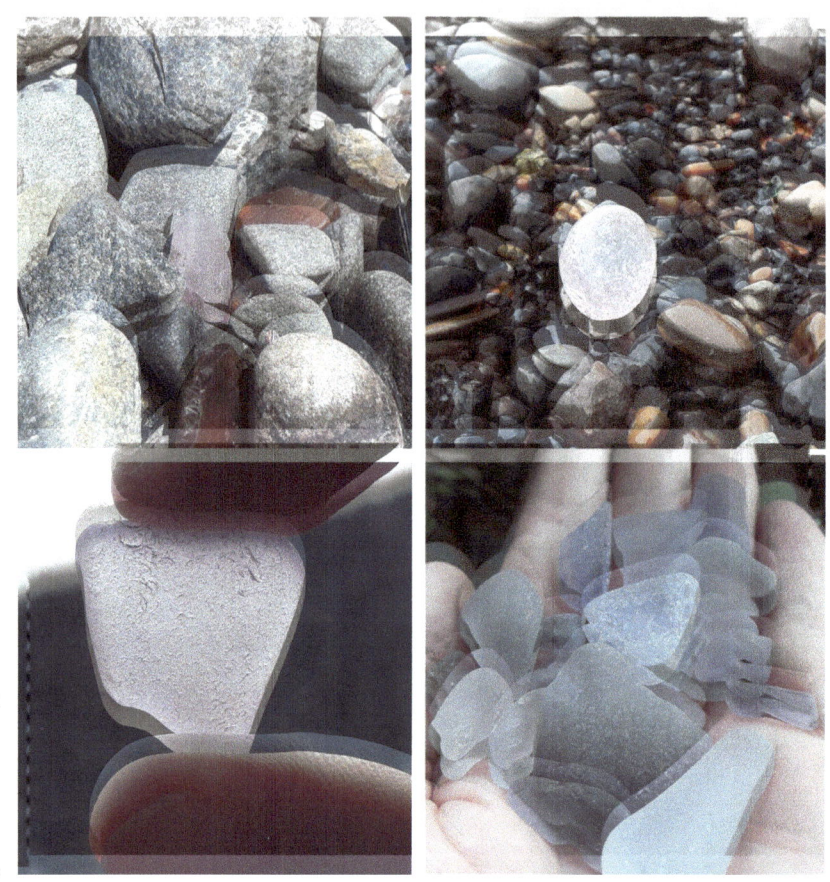

Purple, lilac, blue grey, lavender, and pink can all form from manganese glass. Iron in glass can cause a blue green tint, so manganese was added as a clarifying agent. If you are canning, it's good to be able to see the true colour of what you have put up.

Over time, that manganese breaks down in sunlight and can appear lavender.

Sea glass in these colours can also come from New England glass that used black manganese dioxide, which over time and with chemical changes creates violet glass; the older it is, the more ultraviolet exposure it has had, and the deeper violet the colour becomes.

You can see why people go a little crazy for these rare beauties! They can stand out like bubblegum and other times look like a dusty old bit of quartz, so easy to overlook. You really have to let your eyes take their time roving, if you want to find them.

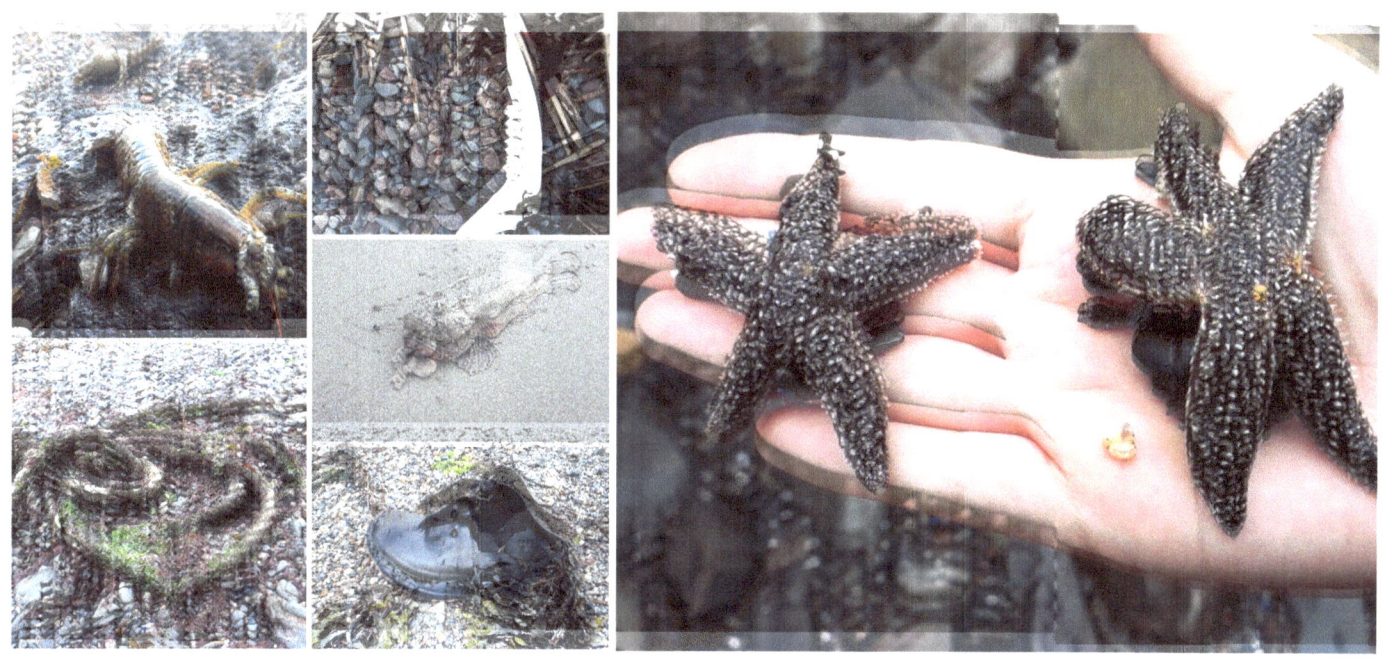

Rocks are pretty amazing, and I do end up bringing some of those home too, along with shells, deceased critters like crabs and starfish, fossils, driftwood, sea pottery, insulators, bones, teeth, and many more odds and ends. I do not bring home larger creatures, and you do come across these in beachcombing too. Not all of nature is beautiful or fresh smelling!

Even though I would head out with the intention of gathering sea glass, and maybe an elusive sea marble, the truth is I find a little magic in just about everything, and it would all end up in my gathering bag, to be admired and maybe even used some day!

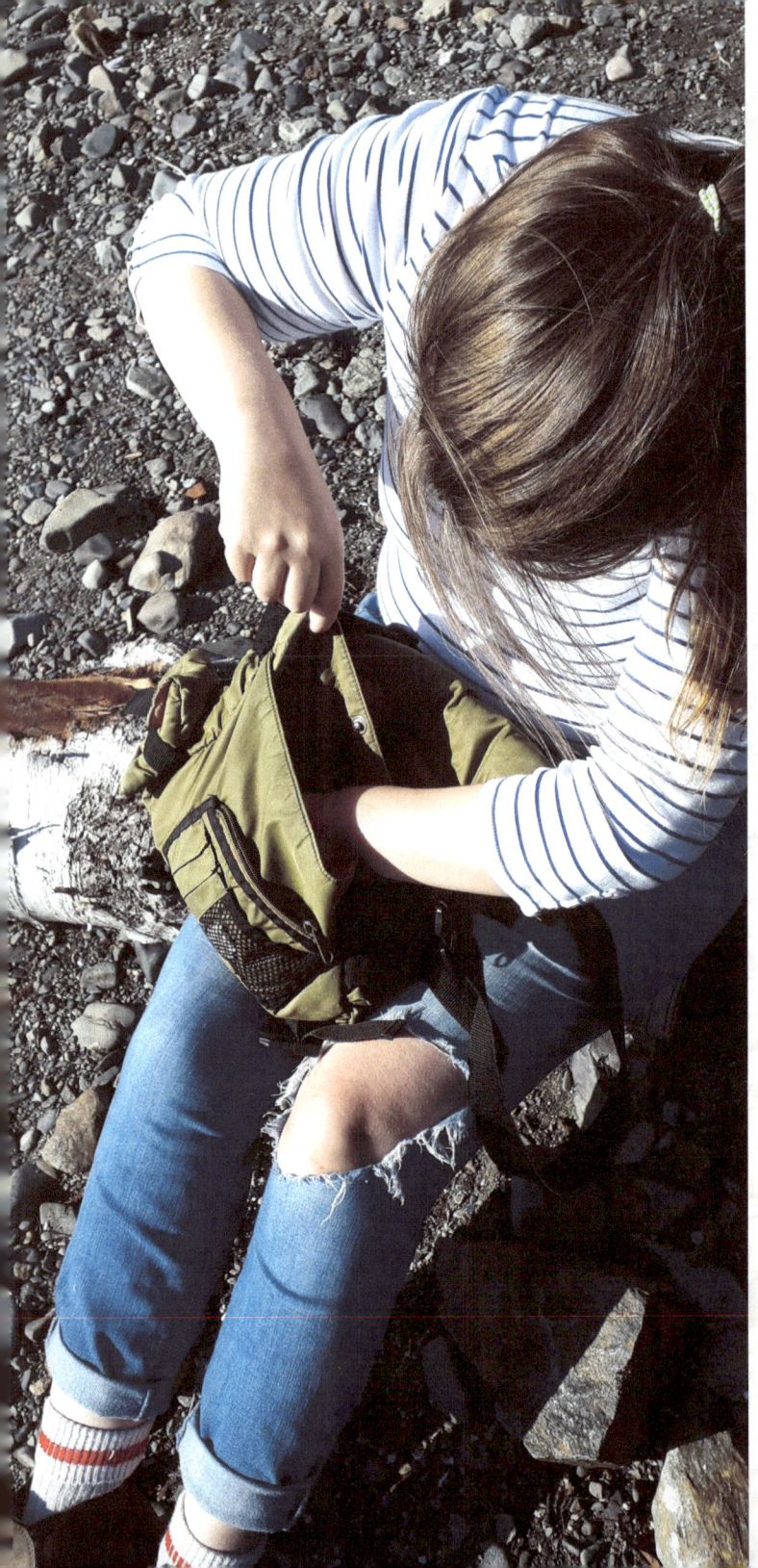

Speaking of gathering bags, a good bag is a great thing. It needs to be washable, fine enough to hold your smallest pieces, yet able to let the water out. It needs to hang low enough to easily reach into so you can safely deposit what you collect.

There is nothing quite like that sinking feeling that comes over you, when you discover that the piece you thought you had, has slipped away somewhere on the journey. Don't forget to give the bag a wash once in a while too, ' l'Odeur de Mer' is a real thing!

It's also handy to have tissues, a bottle of water, sunblock, a hair tie, and a UV flashlight.

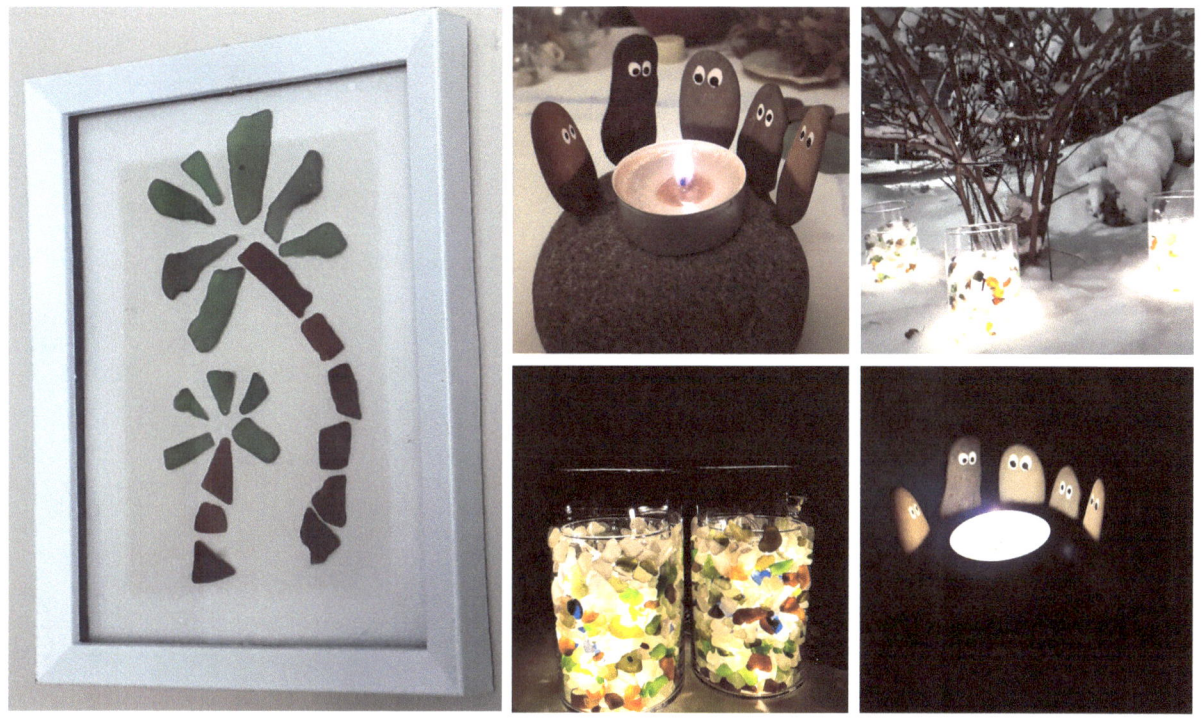

In time, I got a bit better at finding what I was after. Slowly, I got a bit better about making things as well. As a beginner, I stuck with making pictures out of pieces of glass, arranged to look like flowers or trees. I loved how each piece could be so many different things, depending on how you look at it.

The first complete picture I made was of a palm tree, as a gift for my husband, because they are his favourite. I made it on regular paper, and used pva glue. Over time, the sun has bleached the paper, so it looks a bit different, but it basically held up.

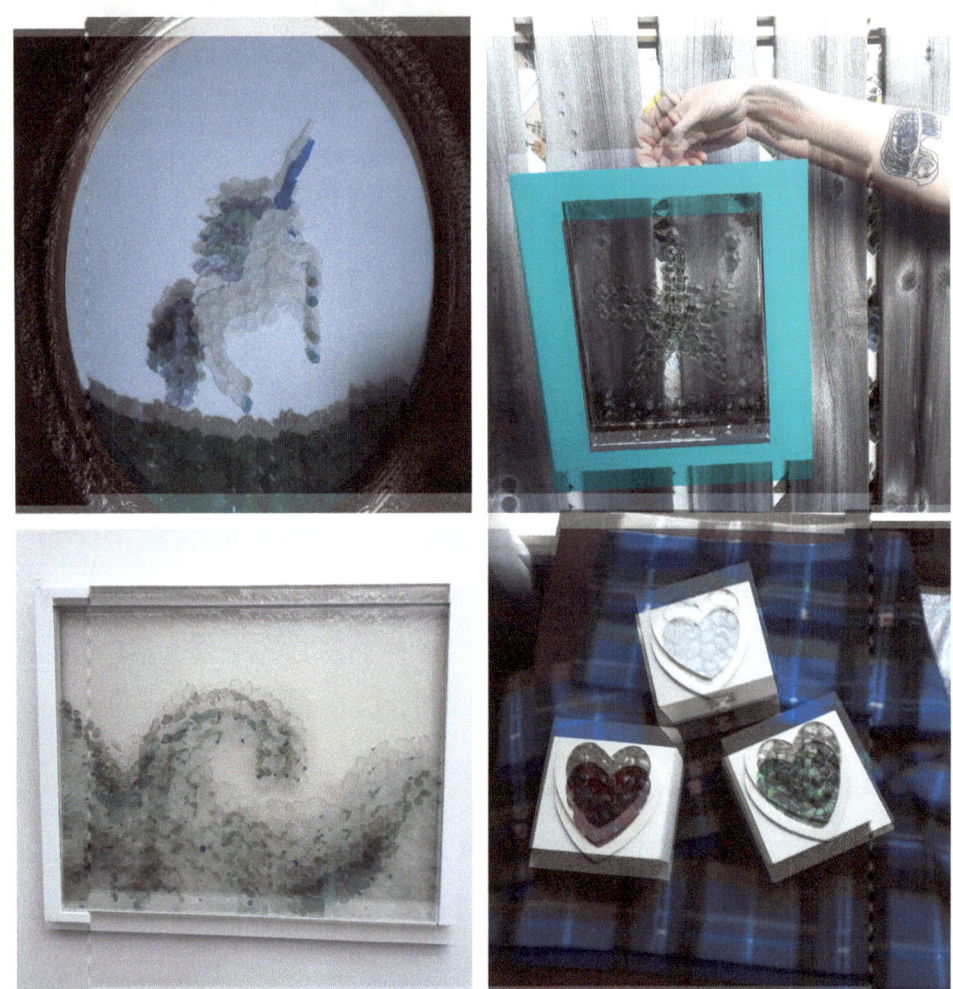

Through asking on Facebook groups and researching on the internet, I learned to use non yellowing glues, and since then, I have created art out of just about every base I could, not limited to watercolour paper, poured acrylic, canvas, driftwood, wood panel, cardstock, egg shells, wooden bowls, linen paper, cotton panel, stone, shells, and bones.

With a strong enough glue, and a bit of vision, almost anything is possible.

Not everything mind you, there was a clay and driftwood mermaid incident that led me through a steep learning curve. To put it simply, clay stuck to wood dries out, cracks, and will break over time.

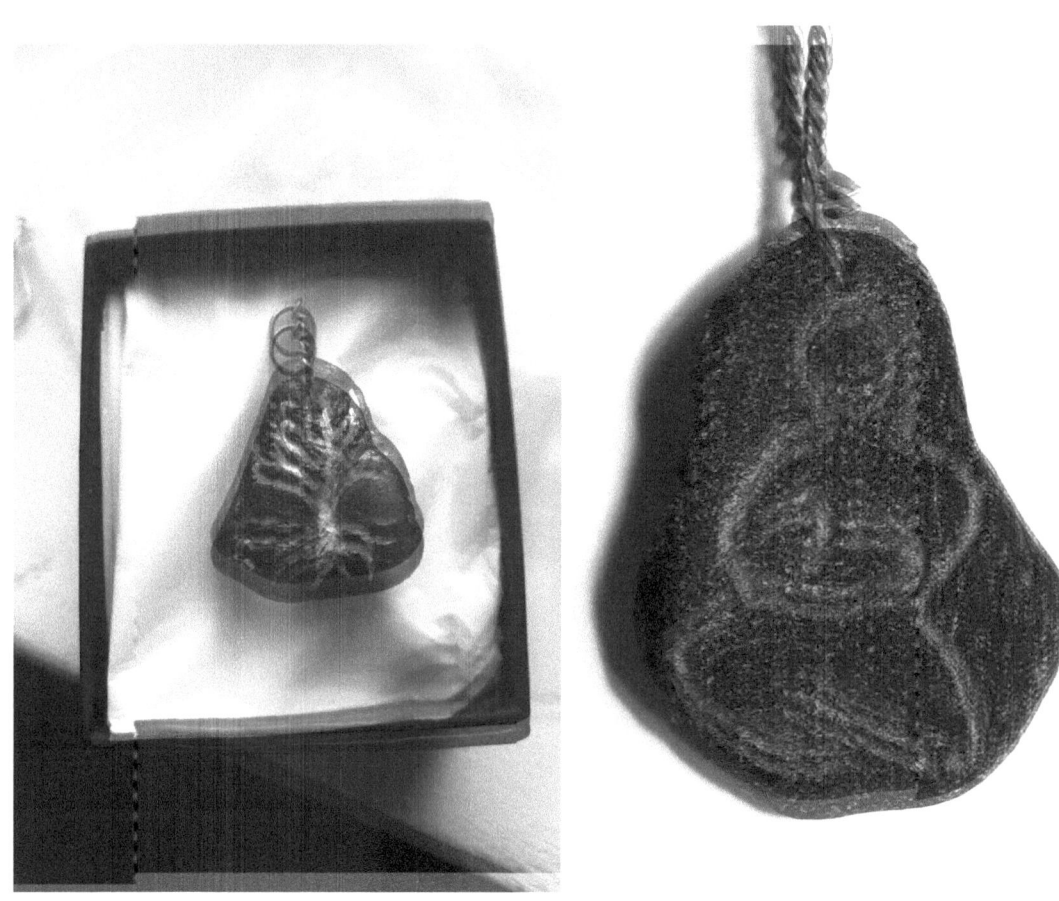

Some people bypass the artsy, craftsy side of it, and B-line to jewellery making. Sea glass lends itself well to it, what with looking like jewels and gems already. It can be made into rings, earrings, bangles, and so much more.

I briefly tried my hand at it, but it wasn't my forte. I do enjoy designing and carving pendants, but I don't have the skills with making rings, wire wrapping, smithing and such.

There are some incredible jewelers out there using sea glass and beach rocks.

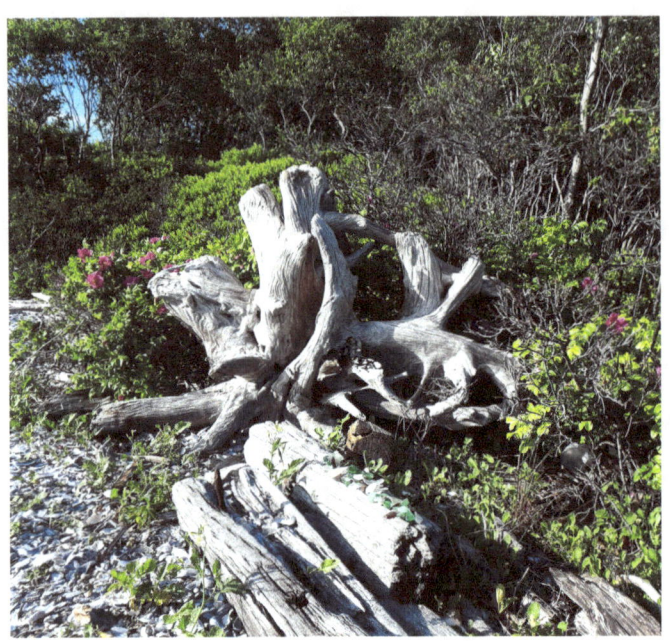 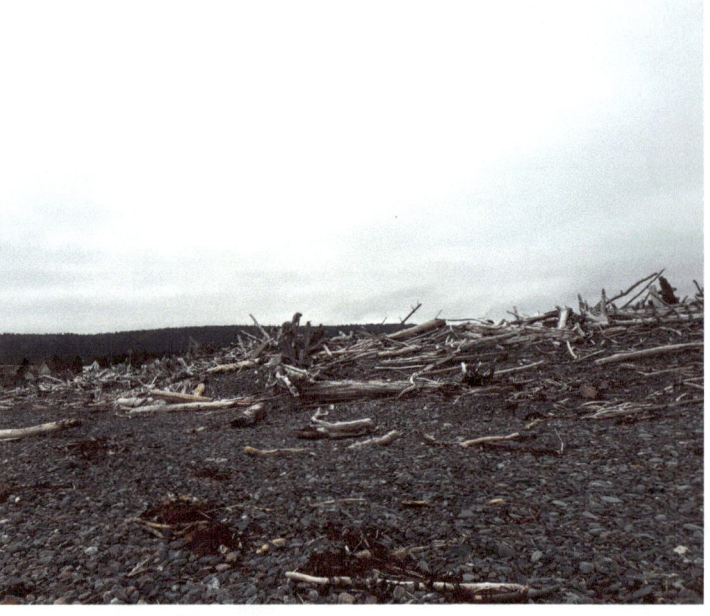

Driftwood is a big thing too, no pun intended. You can end up with huge pieces of driftwood, washed up from storm damage, flooding, old ship wrecks, logging and more. Many already have been shaped by nature and the sea, forming clear objects, creatures, or even letters.

Beaches that occur in shallower areas, facing the sea with a cove or a curve to them, with the right offshore currents seem to get a lot more washing up.

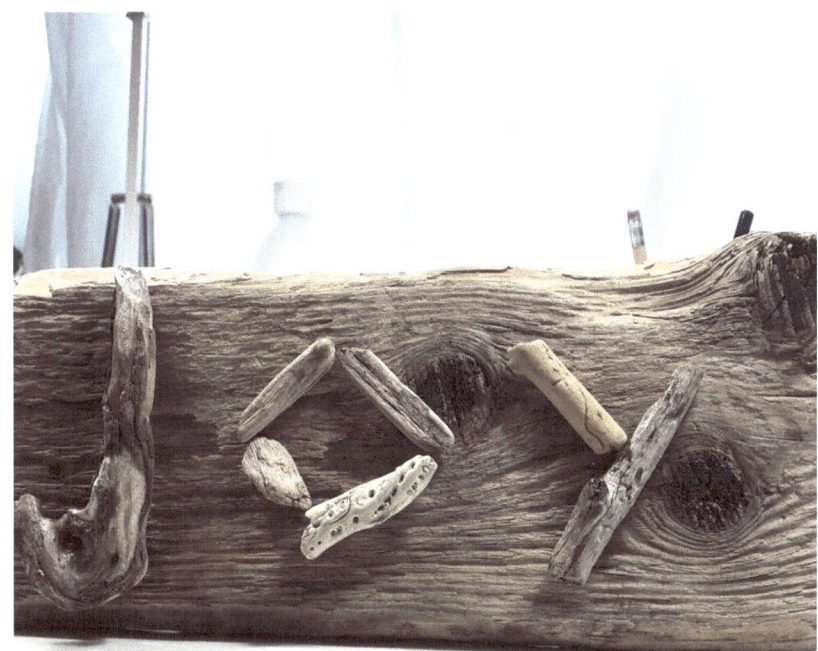
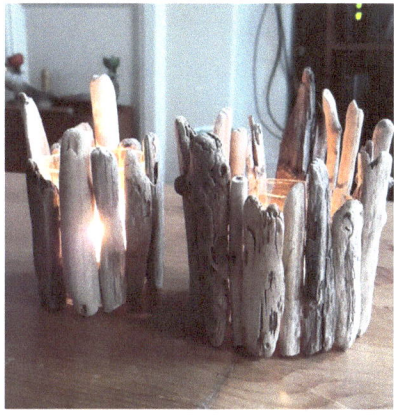
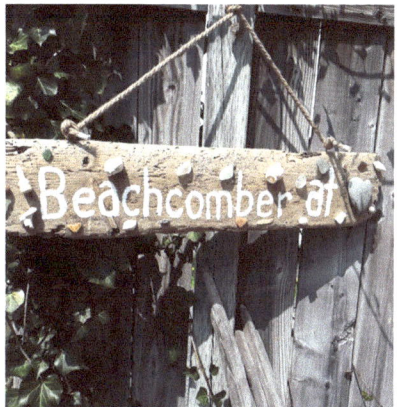
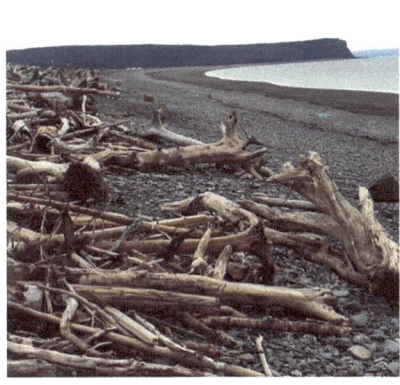
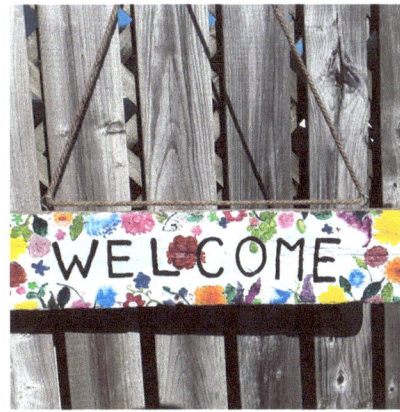
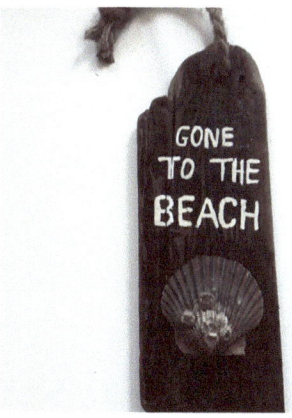

There are so many ways to use driftwood in making art, and I still have a lot more ideas to cross off my list.

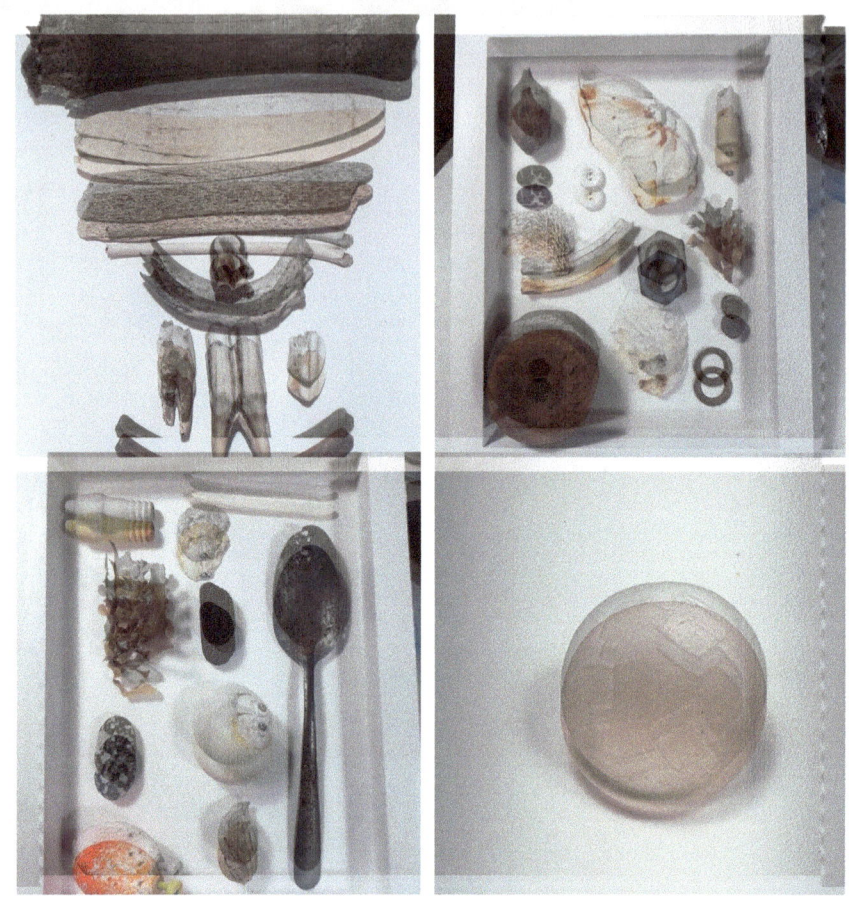

There are a lot of odd man made objects you will find beachcombing as well. Any object, from a paddle to a fork to a belt buckle could be on a ship at the time it goes down. Anywhere mankind has lived for a while, they will make a garbage pile. If it is near the sea, eventually it will end up there.

What I am saying in a roundabout way is; anything can washup, and your preference determines it if is beachcombing treasure or yet more trash on the beach.

I like to bring it all home, sort it out, and they will sooner or later make it into one of my artworks.

I've found buttons, keys, glasses, money, seat belt buckles, carbon rods, shoe leather, clothes line reels, grills, and more.

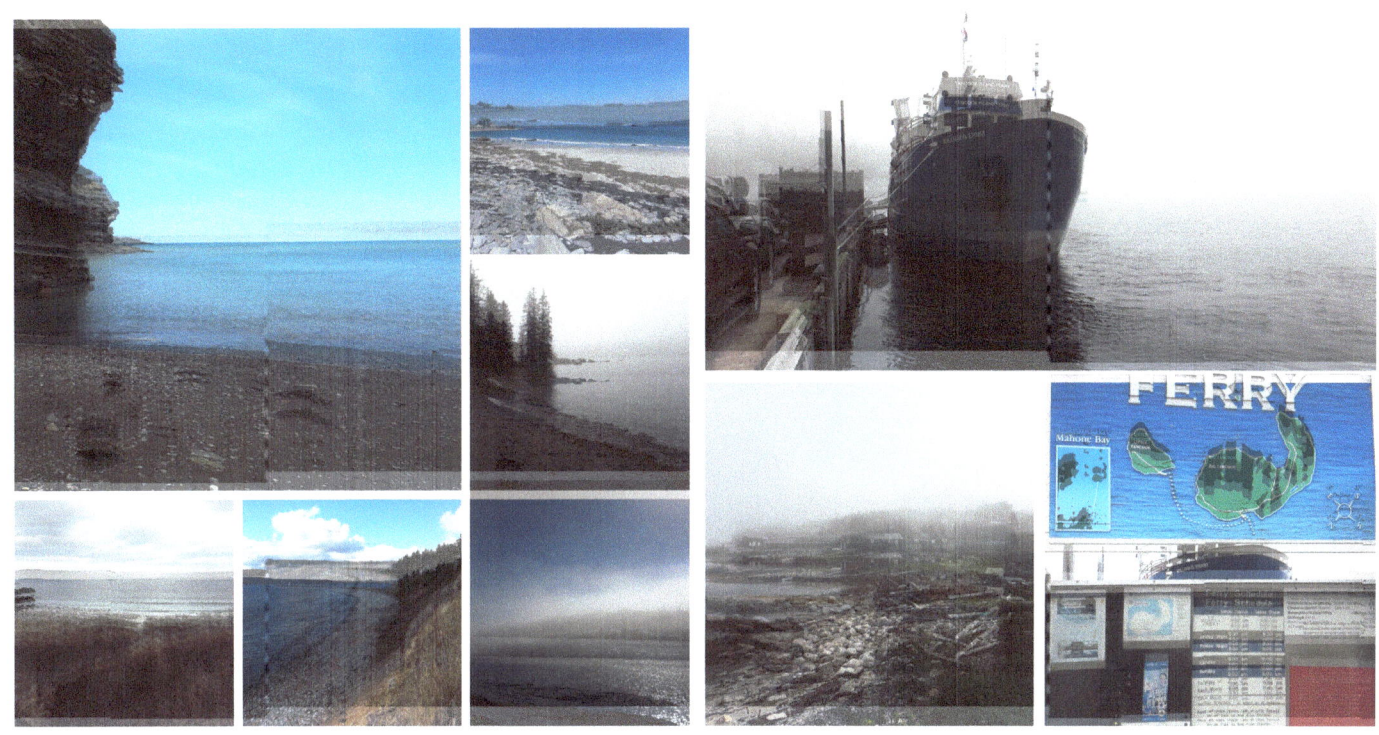

When people ask where I find my seaglass, I tell them all over, because it is true. I travel shore lines, and dirt roads, looking for hopeful spots. I search out local history online, to find where there were once fishing villages, or forts and settlements, and look at old maps. I check out beaches more than once, in different conditions. I read articles about sea glass and join lots of online groups. I ride ferries, or book water taxis. I go out in all weather, all year round and still find many beaches with no glass, or janky sharp glass, along with beaches full of tumbled beauties.

It may take some dedication to find "your beach", but once you do, you'll love it and want to come back over and over.

I know how hard it is to find a good beach, and while I don't have a map of all my favourites, I can tell you some good areas to start your sea glass adventure in Nova Scotia.

General areas good for sea glass are Tancook Island, in the Halifax area around McNabb's Island, Point Pleasant Park, and Eastern Passage, Feltzen South, Brier Island, and in Cape Breton around Glace Bay, Dominion, and Inverness.

Living in Nova Scotia for the last number of years has been an amazing opportunity. Beachcombing, seaglassing, hunting, or how ever you like to say it has been an exciting past time, a chance to explore this beautiful province, meet loads of new friends, and get creative along the way.

However you come to fall in love with sea glassing, I hope it brings you just as much joy.

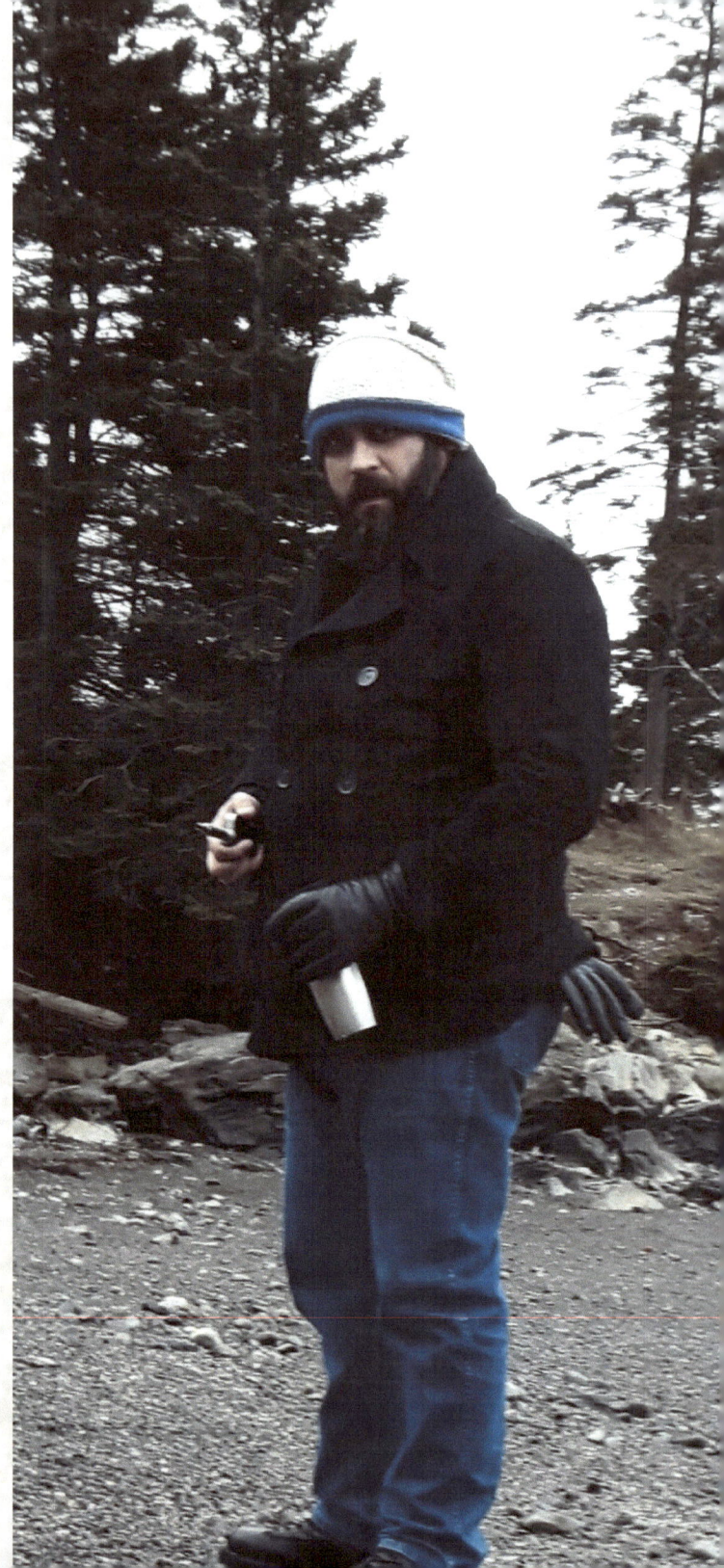

About The Author

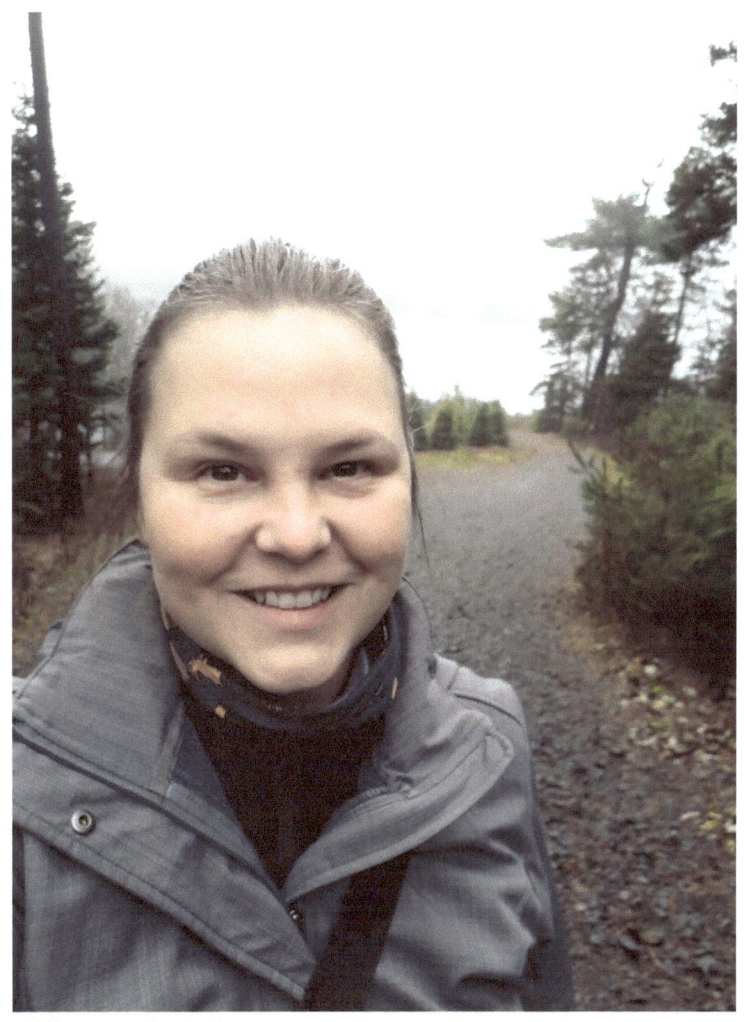

Kristina Noel is a beachcomber artist living in the Halifax area. Working from a small studio, she produces wall art, table lamps, driftwood signs and one of a kind sea life creations.

When not at the beach, she can be found gardening, creating in the kitchen, or exploring back roads.

More From Eaglespeaker Publishing

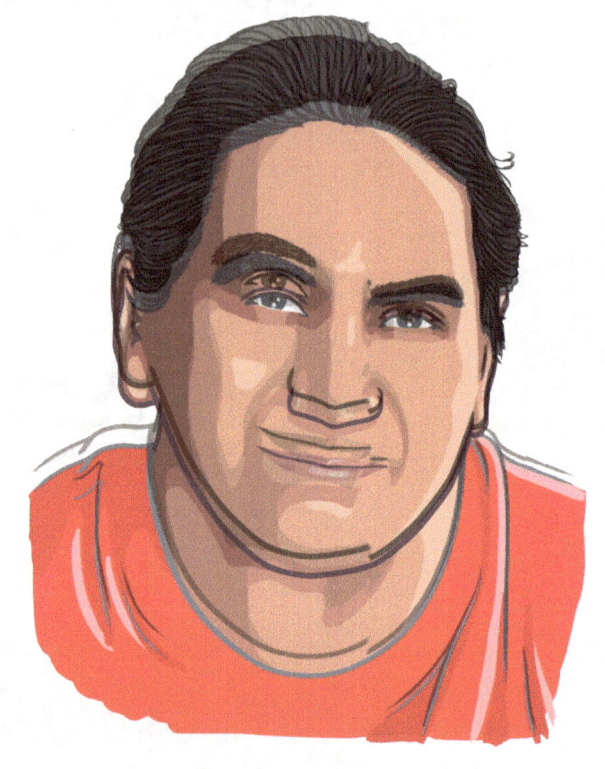

AUTHENTICALLY INDIGENOUS NAPI STORIES:
Napi and the Rock
Napi and the Bullberries
Napi and the Wolves
Napi and the Buffalo
Napi and the Chickadees
Napi and the Coyote
Napi and the Elk
Napi and the Gophers
Napi and the Mice
Napi and the Prairie Chickens
Napi and the Bobcat
::: and many more Napi tales to come

AUTHENTICALLY INDIGENOUS GRAPHIC NOVELS:
UNeducation: A Residential School Graphic Novel
Napi the Trixster: A Blackfoot Graphic Novel
UNeducation, Vol 2

AUTHENTICALLY INDIGENOUS COLLABORATIONS:
Teeias Goes to a Powwow (a series)
Secret of the Stars
Young Water Protector
I Am The Opioid Crisis

... and tons more at **eaglespeaker.com**

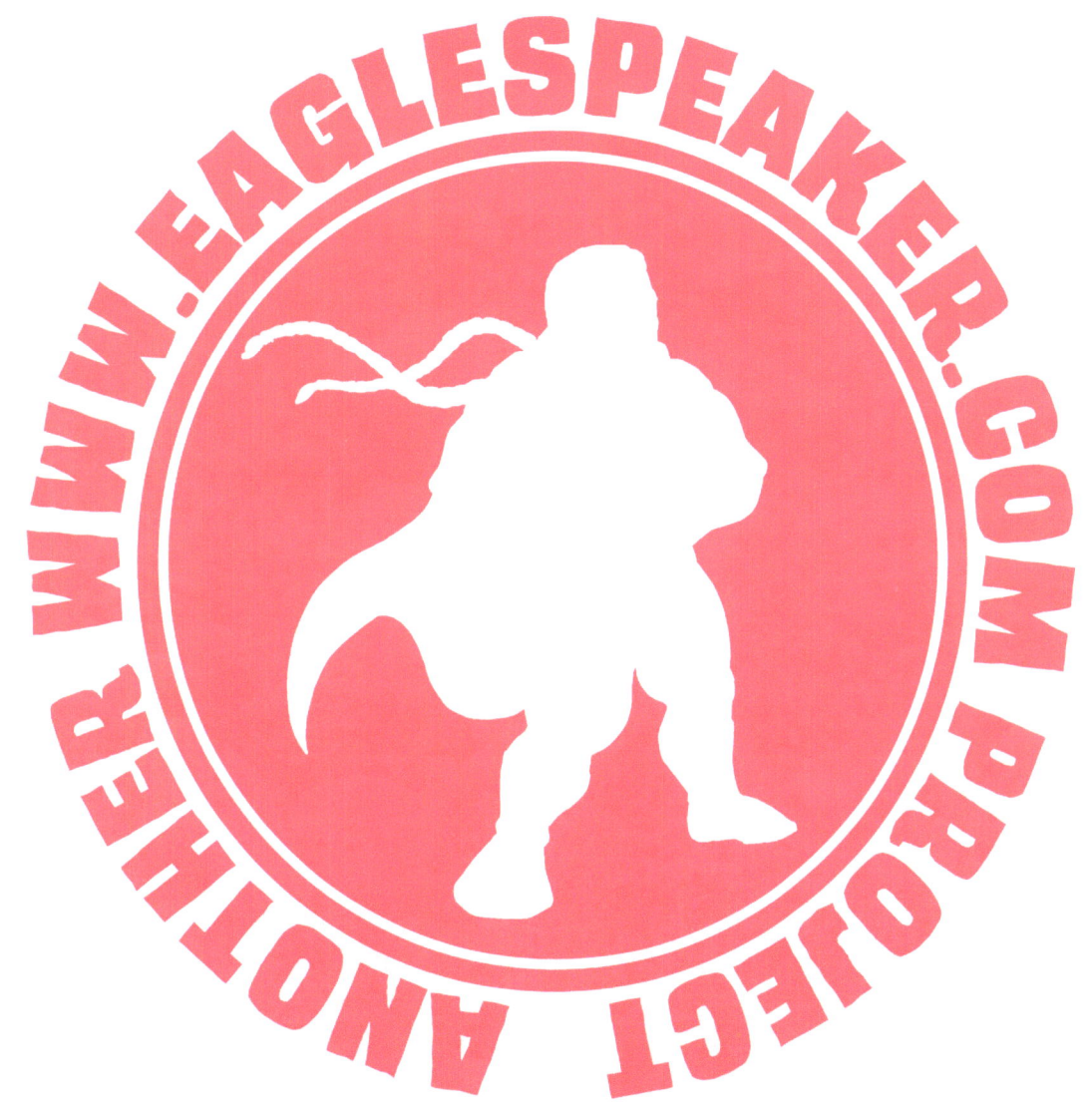

eaglespeaker.com

**if you absolutely loved this book, tell your friends, then find it on Amazon.com and leave a quick review. Your words help more than you may realize.

www.ingramcontent.com/pod-product-compliance
Lightning Source LLC
Chambersburg PA
CBHW051937210526
45473CB00006B/2280